The Price of Truth

Why did they want him silenced?

The Price

of

Truth

By
Mel Pearson

Co-published by Aquila and Trafford
2008

Request for permission should be addressed to Aquila Press, Inc., P.O. Box 252, Noblesville,
Indiana, 46060. This first edition printed by Trafford Publishing.
Co-published by Aquila Press, Inc. and Trafford Publishing.

Note for Librarians: A cataloguing record for this book is available from Library
and Archives Canada at www.collectionscanada.ca/amicus/index-e.html

ISBN: 978-1-4251-8313-4

*We at Trafford believe that it is the responsibility of us all, as both individuals
and corporations, to make choices that are environmentally and socially sound.
You, in turn, are supporting this responsible conduct each time you purchase a
Trafford book, or make use of our publishing services. To find out how you are
helping, please visit www.trafford.com/responsiblepublishing.html*

*Our mission is to efficiently provide the world's finest, most comprehensive
book publishing service, enabling every author to experience success.
To find out how to publish your book, your way, and have it available
worldwide, visit us online at www.trafford.com/10510*

 **Trafford**
PUBLISHING®

www.trafford.com

North America & international
toll-free: 1 888 232 4444 (USA & Canada)
phone: 250 383 6864 ♦ fax: 250 383 6804
email: info@trafford.com

The United Kingdom & Europe
phone: +44 (0)1865 487 395 ♦ local rate: 0845 230 9601
facsimile: +44 (0)1865 481 507 ♦ email: info.uk@trafford.com

10 9 8 7 6 5 4 3

Dedication

This book is dedicated to my life-long partner of 62 years, Adelaide, and to her Dad, William Dudley Pelley. My intimate relationship to both has made possible the writing of this book.

Adelaide made the transition to a Higher Spiritual Plane on November 11, 2005. She was still with me when the expanded draft of "The Price of Truth" had been completed. While we have been separated physically, we have not been separated spiritually, and we will continue the completion of this book collaborating from the vantage point of two distinct perspectives.

In the early 1930s, just out of high school, I became a member of Mr. Pelley's organization, *The Silver Legion,* and subsequently experienced a relationship with him that included espousing the proposals of his book **No More Hunger,** marrying his daughter, Adelaide, spearheading his release from unjust imprisonment, and becoming one of the incorporators of *Soulcraft Fellowship* which published his many esoteric books.

Increasingly, over the years he became my mentor and inseparable friend.

Contents

Photos—pages, 65-81

Introduction

DURING THE 1960s my wife, Adelaide, and I were engaged in the printing, publishing and promotion of the many esoteric books of her Father, William Dudley Pelley. All such effort focused on making the philosophy of life called *Liberation Soulcraft,* or "craft of the soul," as widely available as possible. Tens of thousands of individuals were ordering books and giving testimony to the help they had received in the way of consolment, enlightenment and inspiration in confronting their personal problems of life.

Not totally unexpected, but nevertheless surprising, there arose troubling questions about other areas of his writings and activities not directly related to his metaphysical books. There were many questions about Mr. Pelley's economic and political writings. There were inquiries whether his proposals in **No More Hunger**, outlining a "Christian Commonwealth," were communistic or fascistic.

Was his organization, *The Silver Legion,* brought into being for the express purpose of overthrowing constitutional government? Did he have a hidden agenda to create a society patterned after foreign governments?

And then the question of his imprisonment! Didn't the Federal Government convict him of "sedition" and didn't he spend seven and a half years in prison? This was the most troubling question to them.

The readers were entitled to explanations . . . .

While Adelaide and I knew that the inquiries stemmed from misrepresentations and distortions reflected in the nation's prejudiced media, both voiced and written, it was incumbent on us to explain to the questioners the true picture of what Mr. Pelley stood for and what his economic and political writings and activities represented.

13

This was the genesis initially for our writing a 24-page booklet entitled *The Price of Truth.*

While we gave the briefest picture of his voluminous fictional writings, and his many metaphysical books, the main emphasis was on the persistent attempts to silence his voice and the illegal injustices he endured for his patriotic efforts to make this nation economically just and peaceful. We especially wanted to highlight his efforts to prevent American boys and girls dying needlessly in wars that didn't involve our national security or our public interest.

The book you hold in your hands is an update and more comprehensive coverage of the booklet written in 1961.

Conspicuously engraved across the front of the Supreme Court building in Washington, D. C. are the words, "Equal Justice Under the Law." Every year tens of thousands of Americans visit our nation's capital, are inspired by the implied meaning of this caption, and wend their separate ways confident in the belief that they live in a land where government of law, and not government of men, prevails.

To these Americans the documented case of William Dudley Pelley will prove shocking and disturbing. It will unmistakably demonstrate to them that political trials and political prisoners are by no means confined to foreign lands; that constitutional guarantees of "free speech" and "free press" do not afford protection to the individual who effectively exposes the designs of destructive forces entrenched in society and government; that "due process of law" can be arbitrarily circumvented when illegal conviction and imprisonment of the individual serve the interests of those bent on covering up unhallowed acts.

In considering the Pelley case, we are dealing with the relentless efforts of a fearless writer and publisher who withstood attempted bribes, nationwide vilification, two Congressional investigations and threats on his life in order to forewarn his fellow Americans of the impending dangers to their well-being and security.

We are dealing with sinister forces that do not hesitate to plunge a whole nation into war if it presages regime change, consolidation of corporate globalization and imperialistic dominance throughout the world! We are dealing with incumbent governments that enact legislation that emasculates and destroys the most sacred civil rights of the sovereign citizens.

Strongmen make strong enemies. When such men arise in a nation to unmask the wrong doing of those who exercise usurped economic and political power, they are subject to an unrelenting onslaught, legal and illegal, to silence them. This is the graphic case of William Dudley Pelley. . . .

Chapter One

Who Is William Dudley Pelley?

I WANT TO initially set down several paragraphs giving you a thumbnail picture of my father-in-law and then expand the picture covering the salient areas of his life.

He was born March 12, 1890 in Lynn, Mass, the son of a Methodist minister. He began his writing career as an investigative reporter, working for such papers as the *Boston Globe,* and then subsequently owning several small printing-publishing plants in New England. Later he gained national fame as fiction writer for such magazines as *Saturday Evening Post, Red Book* and *The American Magazine.*

A profound researcher in science, philosophy and religion, he spearheaded efforts for the liberation of human thinking from the gradually increasing crystallization of two thousand years. His application of the original principles of Christianity to religion, politics and economics was so upsetting to the status quo that he was a constant subject of bitter attack by predatory and powerful enemies.

He was an eyewitness to the Bolshevik Revolution and throughout the 1930s led a relentless, nation-wide battle against the treacherous inroads of communist sympathizers here in America. So accurate and authentic were his exposes that only our actual military alliance with the Soviet Union itself in 1942 gave his enemies the war circumstance by which he could be silenced by invoking the wartime "sedition" laws.

He was the victim of an egregious miscarriage of justice. For seven and a half years, 1942-1950, he endured unjust imprisonment. We will present considerable detail of the flagrant injustice done Mr. Pelley at a later time.

From his pen have come millions of words, resulting in over thirty books dealing with philosophy, politics and economics.

One would need to write three separate books to cover even sparsely the three areas that encompass his life. I will cover his literary and philosophical writings quite briefly and then devote the larger coverage to his political writings and the legal travails and persecution that we call "The Price of Truth!"

Pelley's literary career

MOST PEOPLE are quite astounded to find that Mr. Pelley had over 240 short stories published in the best magazines of the time. They appeared in *Saturday Evening Post, Redbook, Colliers* and other slick magazines. He was a constant contributor to *The American Magazine.*

He won the O. Henry Memorial Award for the best short story in the nation for two different years. Several times his stories appeared among the best short stories of the years as edited by Edward J. O'Brien.

Along with his short stories he managed to write half dozen novels, two of which were made into movies, which took him to Hollywood to assist in their production. One book was the *Fog* which was published by Little Brown and Co. and sold nearly a half million copies. The other book was called *Drag* in which Richard Barthelmess was the leading actor.

In addition to the two books, which were made into movies, he was a scenario writer for a number of years adapting many of his short stories into films.

After my father-in-law was released from prison in 1950 up until he passed on in 1965, I shared with Adelaide the unique role of intimate contact with him. I was shop foreman working with him in the printing of his many books and Adelaide did the major proof reading. I also had the interesting role of being his

18

chauffeur on the many trips to the nation's capitol and other destinations.

During those trips I learned of his acquaintance with many of the leading stars while he was in Hollywood, such as Mary Pickford, Gloria Swanson, William Boyd, Wallace Beery and others. His closest friend was Lon Chaney who many of you may remember starred in the "Hunchback of Notre Dame." While working together in New York City, the Chaneys and the Pelleys were social friends.

Adelaide remembers her unique experience when Mr. Chaney lifted her onto his lap, placed a couple of chocolate cup wrappers in his eyes, and made a little horror show for her alone. During recent years when her Dad's films like "The Shock" and "Light in the Dark," in which Lon Chaney starred, were shown at the Indianapolis Art Center, the audience was quite surprised that someone was present who knew the actor.

Adelaide, of course, was only four at the time. At the later age of eighty-nine, she enjoyed the public recognition that she had personally known the actor of a "thousand faces."

It was because of Mr. Pelley's writing achievements that high dignitaries of the Methodist Church made a contract with him to encircle the world and make an assessment of foreign missions. When he arrived in Japan, a violent revolution was aflame in Russia, Czar Nicolas II and his family had been brutally assassinated, and the bloody rampage for usurped power was taking place.

The United States joined with other countries in what became known as the Siberian Intervention. There was real concern as to how far the Red Revolution would spread in its avowed goal of gaining world domination.

Mr. Pelley dropped his writing assignment, joined the American forces, was given a military ranking of second lieutenant, and traveled some 5,000 miles into the heart of Russia on the

Siberian railway. He witnessed first-hand the bloody take-over by Communism.

The experience left an indelible scar on his mind and soul and was to have a compelling influence in his later stand against the recognition of Stalinist Russia during the 1930s.

Before getting into the political sequence in his life, which is of course the prime purpose of this book, I want to cover another aspect of his literary career that is totally non-fictional. It stemmed from a psychical experience he had that led to a lifetime effort of proselyting a fresh and unique philosophy of life that eventually was called *Soulcraft.*

The whole sequence was spiritual in essence and application, and had prominence in his life until he passed on in 1965.

Chapter Two

"My Seven Minutes in Eternity"

HAVING become frayed with his life in Hollywood and repulsed by the immorality and the leftist leanings of the whole film industry, Mr. Pelley sought meaningful respite. His need was solitude and freedom from the hustle and bustle of city life. He needed space and time to correlate and explore certain questions that were gnawing in his mind and were crying for explanations.

Then one night in May, 1928, while living alone in Altadena, California, he had the "psychic experience0" which was to change the course of his life dramatically and set his feet on the true course for which all of his previous achievements had been but training. During this experience, in which he retained full consciousness at all times, he left his physical body to visit higher realms of existence, returning to it later on the same night, greatly shaken and changed.

At the insistence of a close friend connected with *The American Magazine,* he wrote up this unusual occurrence, and it was published in the magazine in the March, 1929 issue under the title "My Seven Minutes in Eternity."

Introductory comment appearing in the magazine stated the following:

> **Not long ago William Dudley Pelley came into the office of *The American Magazine*, after an absence of more than a year.**
>
> **"Man, what's happened to you?" asked the editor. "Your're looking incredibly better than you did last time I saw you."**
>
> **"You've never seen me before," replied Mr. Pelley.**
>
> **"Just what do you mean by that!"**

21

"I mean that the fellow who is standing before you now is a new Bill Pelley---so new that he's only about one year old. I've had an experience. . . ."

On the strength of that conversation Mr. Pelley was asked to write about his great adventure. Neither the editor nor any member of the staff knew what transforming experience the author had been through, but it was evident to all that he had greatly changed, both in appearance and in manner. The accompanying article is the intimate account of his "rebirth." It will surprise and interest you as such as it surprised and interested the staff of *The American Magazine.*

--- The Editor

The sudden, unexpected and overwhelming response to this article shook up the magazine thoroughly, and caused Mr. Pelley to come back from the West Coast to handle the torrential correspondence that was pouring in. He found himself at the start of a decade of whirlwind action. Thousands inundated the magazine with questions and interest. Many related similar episodes that Mr. Pelley had experienced but had been reluctant to tell anyone about them.

Shortly after his "Seven Minutes" experience in May 1928, he discovered that he was able to "tune in" clairaudiently to sources of information above the mortal. He began the "recording" of messages that later were to fill 908 pages in the book entitled *The Golden Scripts.* At the same time he received material less poetic but highly metaphysical in nature which he published in books and magazines.

During this period he was led into an intensive investigation of metaphysics, mysticism and ESP (extra sensory perception) and became engaged in lecturing on esoteric subjects. While in New York City, he published his findings in a magazine called *The New Liberator.* At the same time he organized study groups in the major cities of the nation. Each week he provided lessons to be read by a leader. In Chicago one hundred interested citizens met each weekend to study the unique metaphysical material that they were receiving.

Soon after, he opened a center in Asheville, N. C. called "Galahad College" where students gathered from all over the country for philosophical study.

Chapter Three

What is Soulcraft, anyway?

IN ONE SENTENCE, Mr. Pelley described it as follows: "A different' course of study premised on the theorem that Man first discovers the universe; then he discovers God; then he discovers himself; then he discovers society as sentient material for human betterment."

If philosophy is a collection of basic fundamentals by which Human beings live, then Soulcraft can be called a practical philosophy.

It offers both spiritual ballast and tangible guidelines for the mortal experience.

Many students describe it as a brand new perspective on the engrossing mysteries of birth, life, death, and the realities of Spirit.

Others have described it as an uncovering and a recovering of ancient truths, long lost, or forgotten, or perverted, up the centuries.

Actually, Truth being eternal, there is no question of time involved. Besides, what concerns one is getting sensible answers to questions right now about life's purposes, or about the problems that are continually being heaped upon one, or about one's own relationships with family, friends, community and the Universe. This, Soulcraft had done for thousands over the years.

From the appearance of "My Seven Minutes in Eternity" article in March, 1929, until the last issue of Mr. Pelley's own magazine, entitled "Valor" in June, 1962, a veritable fountain of consolation, instruction and inspiration poured out of his typewriter, providing thousands with their first glimpse into the Eternal Verities, broadening their understanding of Life's purposes and enhancing their spiritual concepts.

When he passed over to the Other Side in June, 1965, he left over two dozen volumes of invaluable teaching, easily read, profoundly moving and personally applicable to every mortal being who walks this confused and turbulent earth, caught in the birth pangs of the Aquarian Age.

What constitutes the Soulcraft library?

FIRST, we have the great compendium of direct messages from the one who calls himself the Elder Brother, which Mr. Pelley recorded and which is known collectively, as **The Golden Scripts.** 908-pages are set down in poetic, Biblical prose, in symbology, psalm and parable in a single book. It has become synonymous with the Bible to many persons who relate to the Elder Brother personally and with indelible conviction.

In recording the supernal messages Mr. Pelley asked if one sentence could be stated that would capture the essence of all the messages. This is what he recorded: *"That every life, no matter how humble, no matter how tragic, no matter how broken and thwarted, hath an inner meaning and is precious in the Elder Brother's sight."*

Then, there is a set of twelve volumes, each containing 13 lectures, that is called **The Soulcraft Scripts.** Each of these lectures (a total of 156) is made up of a direct message received by Mr. Pelley from mentor minds on the Other Side of Life, together with his own comments and interpretations, with an appropriate Mentor Message added. Each of these Scripts may be read by itself with much to be gained, although it is true that more will be gained by reading them in sequence.

We now come to an additional ten volumes each of which will be described with a mere sentence.

As Thou Lovest --- Jesus' life through the eyes of Peter, giving dramatic new perspectives.

Behold Life --- A panoramic view of the whole Soulcraft philosophy.

Thinking Alive --- How substance grows from thought and how thought controls substance.

Earth Comes --- A lively discussion of our planet's relationship to Cosmos and ourselves.

Star Guests --- The Great Migration from Outer Space; the story of "the sons of God."

Adam Awakes --- New perspectives on Romance and Sex in modern life.

Know Your Karma --- How the laws of Cause and Effect affect your current life in mortality.

Getting Born --- How you control your own Birth and your own Life Pattern.

Undying Mind --- On the eternal power and endurance of your individual consciousness

Why I Believe The Dead Are Alive --- WDP's story of his ESP development, sometimes humorous, sometimes dangerous, always engrossing.

In the economic area he wrote **Nations-in-Law,** delving into the ramifications of politics, law and government and the relationships and impact of each in society.

We have already alluded to **No More Hunger** as a blueprint for a better social order based on the principles of absolute justice, in which every individual has equal opportunity to develop his or her inborn talents to the maximum. It will be of importance when we consider the efforts to silence Mr. Pelley.

Chapter Four

Pelley's life takes a drastic change

UP TO THIS TIME, Mr. Pelley had not engaged in political writings of any kind. As a fictional writer of national note, with a lucrative income, there was little inclination to change pursuits in life. However, circumstances were to dictate otherwise. It came about when the major studio he was working for gave him the writing assignment on a short that was being made for the State Department.

This took him to Washington where be became a close friend of Bob Sharp of the Secret Service who was really his boss when he was traveling in Russia. He also became a good friend of Dr. Strath-Gordon who was at one time the head of the British Secret Service. These two men, along with Congressman Louis T. McFadden, who was chairman of the House Banking and Currency Committee, were alarmed with what was transpiring in the United States in the way of destroying the independence of the American people.

While Communism had been forced on the Russian people by terror and murder, a more subtle strategy was taking place in America. It was a process of "government by reaction". Powerful, economic and financial entities were creating the severe, intolerable conditions that were making it natural and "acceptable" for the Administration to step in with all of its relief and subsidy programs. The hidden agenda, and intent, was the destruction of the people's independence and their subservience to "Big Brother" government.

It was inevitable that the nation would succumb to the instability and hardships of the depression years of the 1930s. The tragedy lay in the fact that a bewildered and suffering people little understood the underlying causes of 15 to 20 millions unemployed, tens of millions ill-fed, ill-housed and ill-clothed and a persistent onslaught of foreclosures on homes, businesses and farms.

The contradictory circumstance existed of millions in want, children going to bed hungry, amidst store shelves overloaded with food! It was an enigma that must be challenged!

It was during the Great Depression of the 1930s that Pelley, along with Congressman McFadden, for ten years the chairman of the House Committee on Banking and Currency, launched a documented expose of the privately owned Federal Reserve System. Underscored, were its ties with the financing of both political parties, and how under the guise of "free enterprise" the economy became stagnated and the wealth of the nation was inexorably becoming concentrated in the hands of the few. The vast majority became increasingly burdened with taxes and indebtedness.

It should be noted that Congressman McFadden, on May 23, 1933, formally sought the impeachment of the Federal Reserve Board and its agents and charged them with having unlawfully created claims against the United States Treasury to the extent of over $80,000,000,000 **(80 billion dollars)** in the year 1928 and with similar thefts in 1929, 1930, 1932, and 1933, and in years previous to 1928.

McFadden labeled such egregious and unconscionable theft *The Greatest Crime in History!*

Mr. Pelley could not permit such "sacking" of America to go unchallenged and knew that he must spearhead an unrelenting effort to expose what was happening to an unsuspecting people. His main focus was on the private control of the nation's money and credit and how the major economic abuses and political chicanery stemmed from that unconstitutional control.

No injustice was so small or no conspiracy so big that it escaped his vitriolic and scouring pen, nor his organizational efforts.

30

However, in the eyes of those who would subvert and pillage humankind, Pelley was to commit the unpardonable sin. It was one thing to expose and indict the mischief-makers in society, the debauchers of all that is moral and wholesome, the usurpers of the people's money and government. It was even tolerable that sincere patriots band together in organizations.

But it was neither tolerable nor to be permitted for anyone to expound and promote those solutions for a nation's ills that would bring an abrupt halt to all forms of corruption, exploitation and the devastating role of the privately-controlled central banking system.

A citizenry in distress must not be rallied behind a leader promoting such remedial measures as would place in the hands of the people absolute control and direction of their own economic, cultural and political life. In his book **No More Hunger** Pelley presented for the people's endorsement, and installation, just such remedial measures for the resuscitation and rebuilding of America!

From the standpoint of those entrenched in power they were faced with an enigma. Through their controlled press and radio they could smear and distort Pelley's reputation and activities but attacks, however cunningly devised, against a blueprinted program might be fatal.

It could well boomerang by causing a curious public to procure copies of **No More Hunger** and find that "Red-baiter" Pelley was not only falsely accused of "tipping over existing institutions" but was actually constructively engaged in promoting those safeguards and reforms, all within the framework of the Constitution, that would insure true exercise of both economic and political sovereignty by the people.

Mr. Pelley had a dual role. First, was to expose those who exercised monopolistic and abusive power. Second, was to simultaneously present proposals that would set the nation aright. In order to achieve success in both areas he saw the need to create an organization of patriotic men and women across the width and length of the nation who would share and work for both goals.

Thus the "The Silver Legion" was organized in 1934. **No More Hunger** and its proposals became the central goal of the organization and **Pelley's Weekly** became its official organ for reaching the public. Under the banner of "For Christ and Constitution" individuals joined "Councils of Safety" to endorse and support Mr. Pelley's courageous stand.

Antagonists to Mr. Pelley's organization made undue emphasis on the fact that members were called "Silver Shirts" and thus they related to European "shirt" organizations.

They ignored, of course, the fact that **The Silver Legion's** proposals were primarily for peace and fairness in *our country,* and placed in the hands of the sovereign people absolute direction of their economic, cultural and political destiny.

I, personally, am proud to this day that I became a member in 1936 and proudly wore a gray shirt with the scarlet-red "L" standing for Love, Loyalty and Liberation.

Adelaide is equally proud of her editorship of the **Silver Ranger** during the early 1930s in which she spearheaded the realistic proposals of the "Christian Commonwealth".

Chapter Five

The Smear Technique

DURING the "Great Depression," of the 1930s, we were a nation dominated by a prejudiced press, beholden to monopolistic entities, which unleashed its poisonous venom on Mr. Pelley. The most persistent purveyor of smear and character assassination was Walter Winchell, nationally known Jewish radio personality and newspaper columnist.

Sunday night after Sunday night his broadcasts were devoted to a constant reference to Pelley as a "Nazi" or "Fascist" leader of the "un-American Silver Shirts". He portrayed him as a "fanatic" engaged in "Red-baiting," surreptitiously trying to "undermine American institutions," and a "bigot" who mercilessly sought the extermination of the Jewish race.

At a later date, it was this same Winchell who was to brazenly boast in his syndicated column of November 10, 1947:

> I thawt I'd bust a blood vessel when I read where J. Parnell Thomas claimed he sent Pelley to federal prison and collared Fritz Kuhn. . . Dewey (as D. A.) and his staffers jugged Kuhn, and Pelley (as the Department of Justice will have to confirm) was nobody's baby but ours. . . Where do some of these guys get all that gall! ?

Even the metropolitan newspapers, subsidized by racially biased advertisers, joined with Winchell's weekly harangues and the misrepresentations swelled unabatedly. Only the enlightened recognized the whole vicious attack as the technique of utilizing labels to smear and discredit an opposition whose documented claims and charges could not be answered.

Winchell's reference to Pelley's "violent anti-Semitism" is completely out of perspective. I feel compelled to deal with this false characterization despite the circumstance that most people

33

are quick to side with the accuser no matter how vague the "evidence." Understandably, no one wants any person or group indicted solely because of his or her race.

It is true that Pelley did indict certain powerful entities in Jewry for exercising abusive and disproportionate economic, political and financial power. His personal experience in Russia, when he witnessed the inception of Bolshevism, initially lead by a high echelon of Jews, his years in Hollywood where Jews were dominant, his familiarity with Rothschild international banking and political intrigue for centuries, and the setting up this nation's Federal Reserve System under the aggressive spearheading of Paul Warburg, all supported his conclusions

Pelley was aware that no force in our nation impacted so abusively and devastatingly on the lives of the people as that of private banking. He knew that those who controlled the nation's money and credit controlled both the economic and political lives of the citizens.

It was this power that Mayer Amschel Rothschild, the founder of the notorious Rothschild International Bankers, referred to when he boasted, "Permit me to issue and control the money of a nation and I do not care who makes the laws!"

During Mr. Pelley's writings and activities, powerful Jewish organizations such as the Anti-Defamation League, along with Winchell and Jewish publications, left no stone unturned in vilifying Pelley. They deceitfully used the accusation of "race prejudice" and "bigotry" in a brazen attempt to defame his person and reputation.

"American Jewish Political Action Committee"

WE GET an initial glimpse into the power and functioning of this Committee (AJPAC) by reading a book "They Dare to Speak Out" by former Congressman Findley of Illinois. We get the impact of the Committee's role of destroying the political and personal lives of those who are critical of U. S. pro-Israel policy. Such was the case of Senator Percy of Illinois when he was driven out of the Senate. But it isn't just political personalities whose character is maligned.

Marion Ward, professor at Trinity College in Vermont, and an advocate of "Liberation Theology," is singled out. In 1986 I traveled with her as a member of an investigative group to Central America. Marian Ward was always in the forefront focusing on justice and compassion. I can personally attest to the fact that the attempted defamation of this spiritual lady by the *American Jewish Political Action Committee* was spurious and reprehensible.

Israel is the largest recipient of U. S. foreign aid, which amounts annually to around $4,000,000,000 (four billion dollars). It is this exorbitant underwriting that aids and abets Israel's abusive treatment of the Palestinians. The U. S. is further complicit in furnishing the Apache gun ships, missiles and other lethal weapons causing destruction and death.

"The Israel Lobby and U. S. Foreign Policy" by John J. Mearsheimer, Department of Political Science, University of Chicago and Stephen M. Walt, John F. Kennedy School of Government, Harvard University, (March, 2006) is the most definitive and comprehensive Report to be made public as to how U. S. Foreign Policy and U. S. National Security are shaped by the "American Jewish Political Action Committee".

We and other nations have been witness to Israel's forty-year illegal occupation of Palestine. We have been witness to the unconscionable destruction of the inhabitant's olive orchards, indiscriminate bulldozing of their homes, wholesale arrest without "due process" and the traumatizing of a whole nation.

International abhorrence and condemnation of such terror has defanged the broad and baseless charge of "anti-Semitism" when there is honest indictment of Jewish wrongdoing.

We should note the Israeli-Lebanese war! Bush and his Administration were unabashed partners with Israel in the indiscriminate bombing of Lebanon with the total destruction of its infrastructure and loss of hundreds of innocent civilians.

Mathew Rothschild, editor of *The Progressive* magazine, noted that even a Jewish editor could be castigated with the charge of "race prejudice". He had expressed in his magazine moral indignation to Israel's indiscriminate destruction of property and killing of Lebanese civilians. And what were the reprisals for such expressed stand? His publication, excelling in honest and investigative reporting, suffered hundreds of cancellations.

Certainly, we live in a time of history when neither Jewish nor Zionist abusive behavior is sacrosanct or untouchable!

Chapter Six

"Scourge of Cords"

MR. PELLEY was much aware of Jewish financial dominance throughout the last 2000 years. He was aware of the chronological history from the time that Jesus denounced the Sanhedrin and Pharisees, formed a *scourge of cords* and drove the "money changers" out of the temple, up to the establishment of the Federal Reserve central banking system in this nation.

Only those who are historically naïve, or have some self-interest to hide, are unwilling to admit to Jewish dominant role in the origin, ownership and perpetuation of the scourge of private banking. It is focused on here as a background to belie the accusation that Pelley was falsely indicting the Jews solely because of his hate and prejudice.

It is important and relevant to first note the role of the Goldsmith Bankers of the Seventeenth Century who were the progenitors of the deceitful practice of "reserve lending". A Supplement to the House Committee on Banking's book **Primer on Money,** titled "Money Facts" 88th Congress, 2nd Session, September 21, 1964, covers the origin and development of the *modus operandi* of this practice throughout the history of private banking.

And, then, we have the Rothschild's who were financially dominant during the following centuries and still hold sway in Europe, the United States and the world. . . .

A book called **The Rothschilds**, written by Frederick Morton and published by ATHENEUM, New York, in 1962 embodies documented coverage. The writer had personal contact with members of the Rothschild family in doing his research. No one has put in print coverage so candid and comprehensive as that done by Mr. Morton.

On the inside cover we read, "The Rothschild's story begins at the end of the eighteenth century with Mayer Amschel Rothschild, a Frankfurt money changer. From a cramped house in Frankfurt's Jew Street he built a financial empire that his five sons carried to five European capitals and finally to world-wide power."

On page 13 and 14 we read:

Yet here, in a cramped ghetto dwelling, the great Pauillac wedding had its roots. Here, with a yellow star pinned to his caftan, Mayer Amschel Rothschild kept a small store two centuries ago, and married Gutele Schnapper, and raised with her those five incredible sons who conquered the world more thoroughly, more cunningly and much more lastingly than all the Caesars before or all the Hitlers after them.

The person who spearheaded the efforts to set up a central banking system in America, patterned after what the Rothschilds had achieved throughout Europe, was Paul Warburg, son of the prominent Jewish banking family, M. M. Warburg & Company in Germany. We get personal coverage of his role in "The Region," a publication issued in May 1989 by the Minneapolis Federal Reserve Bank. The pertinent article was entitled "Paul Warburg's Crusade to Establish a Central Bank in the United States."

The article is replete in citing Warburg's presence at Jekyll Island when leading financiers debated, and schemed, to craft the Federal Reserve Act. His moving presence and guidance continued when President Wilson appointed him to the Federal Reserve Board.

What concerned Congressman McFadden and Mr. Pelley was that the central banking systems, that the Jewish International Bankers had successfully set up throughout Europe, was the same devilish private banking system of interest-bearing debt that they had slated for America.

38

The projected goal of the Bankers was to realize central banking systems in every nation in the world.

With the passing of the Federal Reserve Act in 1913 they achieved their goal in the United States.

Jews have played leading roles in the functioning of the "Fed" as it is commonly identified. To name just two outstanding Jewish financial leaders we have Barnard M. Baruch during the time of President Wilson and we have Alan Greenspan of recent time under several Presidents.

During World War I, President Wilson appointed Mr. Baruch, on March 5, 1918, to head the War Industries Board. The Board exercised supervision over virtually the entire industrial fabric of the nation with power to commandeer plants, purchase for the Allies, allocate materials, and place contracts. His authority was *the broadest autocratic control ever vested in any individual in the United States.*

An article entitled "Greenspan and the Myth of the True Believer" by Naomi Klein in **The Nation,** October 15, 2007 refers to Greenspan's autobiography *The Age of Turbulence* and his 18 years as to head of the Federal Reserve. She states that most of the debate over his legacy has revolved around the matter of hypocrisy, a man who preached *laissez faire* repeatedly intervened in the market to save the wealthiest players."

Greenspan referred to "parasites who persistently avoid purpose or reason, perish as they should." Klein states, "Was it this mindset that served him well as he supported shock therapy in Russia (72 million impoverished) and in East Asia after the 1997 economic crisis (24 million pushed into unemployment)?"

The decisions of Allan Greenspan, as chairman of the Federal Reserve Board, have been much publicized of recent years. The ramifications of interest juggling, relating to the ill health and solvency of the nation, are much of public record.

For nearly 20 years Alan Greenspan was the champion of capitalism's predatory "free market" and the preservation of the nation's exploitive central banking system!

Only an enlightened and aroused citizenry will ultimately break the shackles of an unconstitutional private banking system that holds them perpetually in bondage.

Chapter Seven

Jewish Extended Influence

THE INFLUENCE of Jewish individuals, outside of private banking, in the critical affairs of this nation, is well known. The only purpose in this sketchy coverage is to underscore the existence of abusive Jewish influence in other areas in order to mitigate the charge of "anti-Semitism" the instant their roles are identified.

A major political influence has been Henry Kissinger, who during the past 40 years, moved in and behind successive Administrations shaping American foreign policy. He was Security Advisor 1969 under President Nixon and President Ford. Serious charges have been alleged as to his role in the assassination of President-elect Allende of Chile.

And in Christopher Hitchens' book "The Trial of Henry Kissinger" (VERSO, London and New York, 2001) it is alleged that his dilatory action, when Secretary of State, caused the unnecessary death of tens of thousands of American servicemen in the Vietnamese War.

Kissinger, and his associates, constantly have had ties to the highest levels of government.

Other Jewish individuals, holding high office, have also exercised dominant roles in formulating United States foreign policy. Along with other non-Jewish individuals, equally culpable, they are identified collectively as the "neo-cons" who have for years been dominant in Washington.

They are the moving group that let to the fiasco in Iraq, so devastating in needless sacrifice of lives and the wealth of both countries.

For the past twenty years the nation's foreign policy, called the "Project New American Century," has tragically been shaped to make all nations subservient to the United States. This imperialistic project, employing "unilateral preemptive strike," has sought not only transnational corporate control of the world but also ownership of it. It capitalized on Bush's messianic complex to be the front man, with Vice-President Cheney and Secretary of Defense Rumsfeld as willing surrogates for the transnational corporations.

The chief architect of this inevitable fatal Project was Paul Wolfowitz, Deputy Secretary of Defense. He was continually in the forefront promoting for the invasion of Iraq and initiating the strategy for other untenable moves that were detrimental to the United States.

Parenthetically, it should be mentioned that Wolfowitz of recent time was appointed to president of the World Bank. It, along with the International Monetary Fund, has blatantly exploited undeveloped countries for the benefit of the nation's commercial banks during the larger part of the past Twentieth Century. Later he was removed as president because of his conduct in awarding exorbitant salaries to favorite acquaintances.

Another prominent Jew, Richard Perele, Chairman of the Defense Policy Board, and close advisor to Defense Secretary Rumsfield, was also belligerently instrumental in the formulating and advancing of the Project. He was a major investor in a number of defense companies and an unabashed advocate to invade Iraq based on deceit and distorted intelligence.

Many books have been written focusing on how Bush and cohorts dishonestly embroiled this nation in the Iraq war. Congress is finally awakened to the reality that we are involved in a "civil war" that is unwinable.

And the American people are demanding "bring the troops home, now!" It is suffice to say at this time that the whole Project is unraveling.

Chapter Eight

Race Prejudice?

I DON'T WANT TO unnecessarily belabor this question of "race prejudice". However, I want to deal with it in a more philosophical way. Perhaps we can then better understand the misrepresentation and baseless charge against Mr. Pelley. Hopefully, we can recognize that it has been a deceitful ploy to discredit him in the eyes of the people he was so genuinely trying to help!

I personally welcome the opportunity to defend my father-in-law against the charges of "race prejudice". I was the president, under three different mayors, of the "Human Relations Commission" of Noblesville, now a city of 38,000. The Ordinance, which I helped adopt in 1969, made it implicitly illegal to discriminate against anyone because of "color, race, religion, gender, or national origin."

During my 30-year leadership, we resolved multiple cases of discrimination against individuals because of race. We encompassed all the major areas of education, employment, housing and public accommodations.

I was also most active on the state level and was an appointed member of the "housing committee" of the State Commission set up by the Indiana Civil Rights Act.

During those years I worked intimately with my father-in-law as foreman of the print shop and was one of the incorporators of **Soulcraft Fellowship, Inc.** that printed and published the many books that I have already covered. We employed Murphy White, a black citizen, who later was a Councilman in City Government for many years. We also employed for many years Benn Lewis, a Jewish commercial artist, who did the multiple color work for the cover Mr. Pelley's magazine, "Over Here."

I am aware that a family member can be charged with bias. But I hasten to state, without reservation, that my father-in-law was neither a "bigot" nor "racist" either in mind or in heart!

People, who are familiar with the dozens of books written by Mr. Pelley, esoteric as well as political, conclusively know his yardstick for indicting anyone, irrespective of race or color, was based solely on the individual's conduct and actions.

In my third book **Blueprint for Survival** (2005) I state as the foremost pillor upon which a good society should be built is: "Every human being is equally important." I quote a pertinent sentence from the prose poem "Desiderata." *You are a child of the Universe, no less than the trees and birds, and you have a right to be here.*

I emphasize, "The right to be here implicitly underscores the right of each to all the resources of this planet, including the airwaves and all the levels of energy, and an inherent right to explore this planet and develop to the fullest all innate personal potentials."

I further write, "It is in the absence of any divine stipulation or cosmic gradient scale that every human being irrespective of color, race, religion, sex, nationality or sex orientation pleads his or her right to equal opportunity. The effectiveness of such pleading is directly related to the existence of social, economic and political rights on the same level as every other person."

When I was president of the *Noblesville Human Relations Committee,* and also active on the State level, I publicly stressed that we were not primarily concerned about Black rights, White rights, Hispanic rights, Women's rights, Native American rights, Jewish rights or Lesbian and Gay rights. We were only concerned about **Human Rights.**

Before me is a copy of a letter, dated April 22, 1969, that Adelaide wrote to Ben Lewis, the commercial artist for our magazines whom I have already mentioned. It gives us a deeper perspective on race relationships. Her response was prompted by his troubling concern over the rioting caused by African Americans in the nation's capital where he resided. With Mr. Lewis being Jewish, it is most interesting to note that three different races were involved in the letter.

Adelaide, in only a few paragraphs, stated in substance and spirit what her Dad, herself, and I hold in respect to the whole troubling question of race. She wrote:

> Your letter does not make me mad; it makes us sad, instead. The world is too full of misunderstanding, as it is. However, since each must follow his or her own brevet, it cannot be helped apparently.
>
> You see, we are quite well aware that there are blacks that plot murder and mayhem upon whites, just as whites have committed murder and mayhem upon them up the centuries. And, of course, the same is true respecting Native Americans, the Jews, the Chinese, the Japanese, and the Vietnamese. Not all whites, of course, are guilty. But let's get one thing straight: No race is lily pure. If we have learned one thing out of full lives with diverse contacts and connections, it is that judgment cannot be passed on whole races.
>
> Individual performance alone is all that matters. And the individual soul will be sole judge of its own soul-increment.
>
> There is one pervasive evil abroad in the world, the lust for power by way of money, because possession of wealth means, by today's perverted standards, the dominance of power. No man is whole who is <u>owned</u> by another, and as is little understood, no man is whole who <u>owns</u> another. This is the power we are confronting and the chips must fall where they may.
>
> "Teach my sheep to go in the right path, the path of absolute justice, each man as it falleth onto him to perceive whereof he would have it measured unto him," say the *Golden Scripts*.

45

It is the goodness, the humaneness, and love, in the heart of man that we seek, regardless of his race, his skin color, or his status in society. Goodness of heart may be found anywhere, strangely enough, more often among the very poor than among the very rich. The principles of "No More Hunger" are not designed for a "chosen" group. They apply to every human being. I suggest you read over Chapter 105 in the Golden Scripts. I may add we are getting used to the "thistles."

It is my turn to say, do not be angry. Also, I say to you, do not judge hastily. What happens to the world is not of account; it is a temporary thing. How the individual soul responds to challenge is the only thing of eternal value.

With good wishes always to you, Mrs. Lewis and your son,

Ever sincerely,

Adelaide Pearson

Before going to the next chapter, I want to make several things unquestionably clear. In indicting the role of private banking, and its horrendous abuses and endless suffering, I am not accusing the personnel working in banks of being accomplices in any way. They are generally courteous, efficient workers merely trying to earn wherewithal to raise a family.

My focus is on the faulty, barbaric system that has existed over the centuries. It is a system that has allowed the exploiting of the hard work of everyone. It has prevented reform of the whole money-credit process that would release the nation's full work capability for the people's well being. It has prevented the realization of equal human rights for every individual and placed the people and the nation in perpetual bondage.

Unfortunately, the private banking system has been surrounded with a veneer of respectability, and with everyone dependent on its services, it has been generally immune from charges and indictment.

46

The guilt and involvement of certain elements of Jewry spearheading and establishing the whole private banking system are well documented. However, we must realize clearly that the main stream of Jewish individuals, hard working, law-abiding and tax-paying citizens are as victimized as non-Jewish persons within the all-inclusive private banking system.

Another relevant point that must be recognized is that in the expose of wrongdoing in this society some of the most active leaders are Jewish investigators like Howard Zinn, Noam Chomsky and editors like Mathew Rothschild of *The Progressive* magazine to whom I referred to earlier.

During the past year, I have been writing a book, entitled *The Scourge of Chords,* which covers chronologically the history of banking in this nation but with much detail and documentation that is lacking in the sketchy coverage in this book.

The best criterion we have in judging anyone, or any system for that matter, is what Christ stated: "By their works ye shall know them!"

Chapter Nine

The North Carolina Litigation

ANOTHER misconception entertained by many uninformed Americans is that Pelley was involved in some sort of "fraudulent stock swindle" in connection with his publishing activities in the State of North Carolina. Tragically, the true facts respecting the forgoing false accusation, along with all other distortions from the Winchells and others, are unpublicized.

Pelley's efforts, from the beginning of the 1930s, were taken notice of by dominant economic and political forces entrenched in the New Deal. They were disposed to resort to any action that would achieve his silence. They didn't have any concrete case to bring against him so they would do anything, legal or illegal, to suppress his writing, publishing and organizing.

The North Carolina litigation, fraught with the maneuverings and deceit of those on all levels of government, including Congress, was the first major attempt to "railroad" Pelley behind prison bars. It had its motivating inception in 1934 in the Samuel Dickstein Committee, purported to uncover "un-American Activities." The Committee sent agents down to North Carolina, which ransacked Mr. Pelley's offices and printing plant, frantically searching for anything that could be used to silence him.

They gloated with glee when they discovered that Mr. Pelley inadvertently had failed to make proper registration with the State Corporation Commission when he moved to North Carolina. It was this "crime" that subsequently, brought him before the bar of justice on a technical violation of the *Blue Sky Laws*.

Judge Wilson Warlick imposed a one-to-two-year sentence for the technicality but would not be a party to stopping Pelley's patriotic efforts by a minor violation. He ordered the payment of court costs and suspended the sentence.

A fifteen-year interminable harassment and persecution ensued before Judge Tom White of the Circuit Court in Indiana in 1950 decided "enough was enough" and ruled against the court in North Carolina.

The Indianapolis Supreme Court confirmed the decision later.

The immediate question arises: "But how could such persecution be prolonged over a fifteen-year period on a mere technical conviction?" Incredible as it would seem, the whole malicious prosecution was continued on the charge that Mr. Pelley violated the "good behavior " clause of the suspended sentence, despite the fact that he had not as much as received a traffic ticket during that time.

The continuous harassing and persecution of Mr. Pelley came about when Prosecutor Zebulon V. Nettles of the original trial later became Judge Nettles of the court. This circumstance provided a vindictive opportunity for former prosecutor Zeb Nettles to personally get revenge in losing the original case.

At the same time it gave satisfaction to the Dickstein Committee that had initially sought to silence Mr. Pelley.

As already mentioned, the trumped up charge was that he had violated the "good behavior" clause of the suspended sentence. He was accused of "demeaning the President of the United States" and being brazenly critical of the policies of the New Deal Administration.

A gentle woman in the State came forth and posted the required $10,000 bond assuring Mr. Pelley's appearance at a later hearing. Mr. Pelley left North Carolina to take care of his business elsewhere. In 1939, he voluntarily appeared before the permanently established "Un-American Committee," headed by

Congressman Dies of Texas, and testified that he was dissolving his organization, the *Silver Legion*, in light of the Dies Committee purporting to do the work that he had been doing.

So ended the 15-year North Carolina desperate, but futile, attempt to silence Mr. Pelley.

How, then, to bring about an end to Mr. Pelley's writings and activities!

Chapter Ten

The God of Carnage Sets the Stage!

EMBROILMENT of this nation in World War II at last furnished the key to lock the prison gates behind the subversionist's chief antagonist!

Pelley was still under the $10,000 appeal bond to North Carolina in 1942 when the Federal authorities swooped down with a vengeance, charging him with alleged violation of the sedition laws. Despite the fact that he was physically confined in Federal custody making it impossible for him to appear in North Carolina on the day commanded, the $10,000 State bond was forfeited. Injustice was already compounding, yet for Pelley, illegalities had barely commenced to get rolling!

When war arrived, in 1941, the sedition laws could be invoked to silence all opposition not only to Communist infiltration in the country but also to corruption in high places. Constitutional rights could be suspended. Government became judge, jury and jailer. No proof of overt acts was required to condemn the accused forthwith to servitude. It was only a matter of making out a nominal case against the individual and war-hysterical juries would unerringly do the rest. They would convict as a matter of reaction, fearing to be tarred with the brush of "abetting sedition."

Thus the majority of the sedition cases which were brought in World War II by the Department of Justice, certainly the Pelley "sedition" case, had nothing to do with counseling men not to fight, or advocating measures which obstructed hostilities. They had everything to do with working vindictive scores against crusading antagonists of the Stalinist way of life and against oppressive government, erasing them punitively with the war as a weapon!

Before the California Bar Association in December of 1941, United States Attorney General Francis Biddle promulgated this purported assurance to all Americans, including Pelley:

> **In tense times such as these, a strange psychology grips us. We are oppressed and fearful and apprehensive. If we can't get at the immediate cause of our difficulties, we are likely to vent our dammed-up energy on a scapegoat. That sort of psychology is the very essence of totalitarianism. On the other hand, civil liberties are the essence of the democracy we are pledged to protect. Insofar as I can, I intend to see that civil liberties in this country are protected, that we do not fail again into the** disgraceful **hysteria of witch-hunts, strike-breaking and minority prosecutions which were such a dark chapter in our record of the last World War.**

That this was pure double-talk was quite apparent to Pelley a few short months later when Biddle's own department awoke him on an April morning in Connecticut and presented a warrant for his arrest!

The day after Pearl Harbor, Pelley had terminated his chief political publication "Roll Call." He had only resumed publication of further constructive criticism after Attorney General Biddle's positive assurance that constitutional rights of free speech and free press would be protected.

The head of the Justice Department, under solemn oath to support and defend the Constitution, had resorted to sheer entrapment!

Chapter Eleven

The Indianapolis Trial

AFTER his arrest on April 4, 1942, and his return to Indianapolis, he was placed under a bond of $15,000, and in June was indicted for violation of Sections 33 and 34 of Title 50 of the U. S. Code, these sections being popularly known as the wartime "Sedition Law." In an atmosphere of war hysteria, with the nation allied with Stalinist Russia, which suddenly overnight had become "democratic," it was but routine to railroad Pelley into a Federal prison.

Legal scholars have consistently recognized that "sedition" is a political crime. Since the passing of the "Alien and Sedition Acts" in 1798, sedition laws have been used by those in power to suppress all who oppose the policies and actions of the incumbent government. So it was when Mr. Pelley was singled out because of his opposition to the policies and acts of war that the Roosevelt Administration was committing that led to American embroilment in World War II.

Later we will be focusing on the book "Perilous Times" in which Professor Jeoffrey Stone, Dean of the University of Chicago Law Department, covers historically the abusive use of "sedition" during wars from the Revolutionary War to the present. It is most relevant to note that he singles out the Pelley Case as the outstanding miscarriage of justice during World War II. He also cites the actual role President Roosevelt played in bringing about Mr. Pelley's arrest and prosecution.

So determined was the Roosevelt Administration in making doubly sure that Pelley was silenced once and for all time that the Justice Department sent two special assistants to the Attorney General out to Indianapolis. One was Henry Schweinhaut who later was promoted to a Federal judgeship for his role in assuring a conviction. The other was Oscar Ewing who after the conviction of America's No. 1 Political Prisoner was appointed to the top position of the Federal Security Administration.

The Pelley trial in Indianapolis was a complete disavowal of "due process of law" and a flagrant disregard of a citizen's constitutional guarantees. His constitutional right to subpoena witnesses in his behalf was arbitrarily limited. Only U. S. Congressman Thorkelson of Montana and Charles Lindbergh, "the Lone Eagle," were allowed to testify in Mr. Pelley's behalf, and both were given restricted time.

The prosecution proved neither the elements of "intent" nor of "clear and present danger", which the Supreme Court held in subsequent cases must be in evidence in order to prove violation of the law.

From beginning to end, the whole procedure reeked with injustice and malicious prosecution. Irrespective of either the law or the facts, powerful influences in and behind the Roosevelt Administration were fanatically determined that Pelley must be silenced. The God of Carnage had set the stage for the Twentieth Century's outstanding purge trial!

As chairman of the "Justice for Pelley Committee" I had many contacts with personnel of both the House and Senate Judiciary, and other relevant Congressional Committees.

I also made a concerted effort to contact all areas of the media. I particularly contacted editors and investigative reporters of leading newspapers.

At the same time, Adelaide launched a nationwide letter-writing campaign to enlighten the public as to the miscarriage of justice dealt her father and to plead for financial help to offset the tens of thousands of dollars in legal fees and printing of court briefs. She also appealed to them to write their representatives in Congress apprizing them of the Pelley injustice.

On August 12, 1942 Judge Baltzell sentenced Pelley to fifteen years in a Federal penitentiary on the charge of violating the wartime "sedition" law, the *1917 Espionage Act.*

Again, as on another occasion in history, a cry arose, "Crucify him, crucify him!" His accusers were jubilant, and the gullible cheered. . . .

But they weren't satisfied in just putting Pelley behind bars. As they gloated about this achievement, they were about the business of "cleaning up the whole Pelley Clan" as reported by Walter Winchell and the daily media.

Chapter Twelve

Pelley's Daughter Arrested

ON THE MORNING, after Thanksgiving, there came a knock on the door of the apartment that was occupied by Adelaide and several co-workers. Six FBI agents appeared at the door and demanded to see Pelley's daughter. They had neither search warrant nor arrest warrant. While two of the agents questioned Adelaide, alleging that she was guilty of "harboring a fugitive from justice," others were ransacking the apartment and randomly boxing up all material that they felt would support their false charges against her.

Adelaide had no time to call a close friend or to contact an attorney. She barely had time to dress and several agents suspiciously accompanied her visit to the bathroom less she try to escape out of some camouflaged window. With the garnered boxes she was whisked off to Indianapolis to be questioned for a whole day before being locked up in the City Jail awaiting formal charges.

At the same time the Agents were grilling Adelaide, on the morning after Thanksgiving, I experienced a strange, and somewhat eerie, "psychic" phenomenon. I lay no claim to being clairaudient. However, in this instance I had definitely "tuned in" to a happening nine hundred miles away. It were as if I were present during the interrogation of Adelaide and emotionally shared the threatening content.

While my brother and I had general plans to go to Minneapolis and be recruited for work at the Kaiser Shipyards out West, I felt a compelling urge, that we should make the trip in double haste. What was the significance of this inner prompting? I only knew that I should heed it.

The night before the holiday I had arrived back to northern Minnesota after working at the construction of a huge military airstrip in Scottsbluff, Nebraska. Walt, likewise, arrived at our home having quit his job for a large construction company. Immediate steps were needed so we could be on our way to Minneapolis.

Did the local banker sense there was something providential about our trip when he so readily agreed to open the bank the day following Thanksgiving to handle the selling of my car?

It was only a matter of hours before we would know the need for the hasty trip.. Something had happened that would deeply concern us. More personally, someone, somewhere, awaited my arrival. There was a compact, which had been agreed upon before our entrance into life, which awaited fulfillment.

After the long bus ride, we went to bed early and arose with the rising of the sun to be first in line at the recruiting station. Our direct trip to the recruitment place was interrupted by a sudden urge to stop in a small restaurant to have a wakeup cup of coffee. At the counter, Walt picked up a copy of the daily paper and commenced to peruse it. On the second page he noted the heading "Pelley's daughter arrested."

She had been brought before a presiding magistrate, charges of "harboring a fugitive from justice" were alleged, bond was set and she was carted off to the City Jail.

Parenthetically, it should be noted that subsequently, some six months later, the contrived charges were dropped. In the interim the anxieties of a prison term and the burden of mounting legal fees were added pressure. When you are targeted to be silenced, the "enemy" uses the harassing technique of bringing charges against you knowing that they cannot be legally sustained but they will exhaust your resources.

What is of special personal interest is the fact that if we had not been prompted to stop into the small diner we would have been on our way to the West Coast unaware of what had happened to Adelaide and her need for help. However, destiny would keep us on the right track. There was a compact to be adhered to and be consummated.

I digress for a couple of paragraphs to set down some perspective as to "compacts" that are made by individuals before incarnating. First, we should accept that this is not a random Universe. It has organization, it can be measured, it operates according to immutable laws, and it has logical purpose.

As incarnated spirit-souls we are integral parts of that Universe. There are no outside boundaries. It is an all-inclusive entity. What, then, governs our sojourn into mortal life? Is it just a hit-and-miss experience? Do we come into life only by the procreation invitation of our parents? Or is there some predetermination as to what should be the principal elements that go into the earthly experience?

Intuitively, along with tapped in knowledge to Higher Sources of wisdom, we come to accept the formulating of "compacts" as to our life plan and what it should entail for our spiritual enlightenment. Who should be our parents, what should be our early background, what are the roles we should play, and most importantly, who should we meet to establish partnerships to achieve our main purpose in incarnating?

Now, back to Walt and my parting. We pooled our resources. Walt left that evening for the West Coast and I boarded a bus for Indianapolis with a reasonable amount of money to underwrite what financial help was needed. It turned out that our help was most timely since not sufficient money had been raised to cover the assessed bond and Adelaide was being held in the local City Jail for extended days.

I met Adelaide as she came down the steps of the Federal Building in Indianapolis. In shaking hands I didn't know quite what to say. I was groping for words. As our eyes met, I knew that I had known her before. It seemed so inadequate to simply say, "I'm sure glad to meet you!" My mind and heart wanted to blurt out "Here we are together again, fulfilling a compact that we made before we incarnated into mortal life!"

At the restaurant on the Circle in Indianapolis we learned of Adelaide's five-day experience in the female section of the jail. It had been somewhat of a harrying experience to be locked up with women, mostly in their teens or early twenties, charged with possessing illegal drugs, prostitution, stealing or abuse of children. At the same time Adelaide found a certain rapport with many. When one reached into their inner minds and hearts they were sympathetic humans who in most cases adverse circumstances had led them to commit unsocial acts.

I told Adelaide briefly of my turn down by the military, my work at the air base and how I had parted with Walt as he headed west and I headed east. In all the conversations there were intermittent moments when she and I would focus on each other seeming to weigh who each really was and what had so abruptly brought us together.

It is sufficient to state that on the way to Noblesville, with the temperature 20 degrees below zero, Adelaide and I shared a blanket to offset the frigid weather. The chilly night little diminished our warm and renewed camaraderie. Later, she confided in me that she felt a strong psychic feeling that as we rode through the night we would be sharing a blanket for the rest of our lives.

This was the backdrop against which Adelaide and I had made a mortal compact that was to be a sixty-two year sojourn on this earthly plane. "The Price of Truth" covers one aspect of our joining hands and minds in striving for her Dad's exoneration and release from unjust imprisonment.

The other efforts involved the promotion of the working philosophy called "Soulcraft" and our goal of bringing about the adoption of a *"National Cooperative Commonwealth"*. All are segments of our earthly compact of working together as a team.

Adelaide graduated to a higher Spiritual Plane on November 11, 2005 with much of our work still unfinished. While we have been separated physically, we have not been separated spiritually. To complete our earthly mission, Adelaide will function from the higher spiritual plane and I will perform on the mortal plane. She will help me from her higher vantage point.

Adelaide has simply gone ahead and I will follow shortly and once again join her when final mortal goals of our compact have been completed.

The anticipation is fraught with joy and spiritual uplift!

Mr. Pelley was sixteen years old when he went to work in his father's factory in northern New York. He became general superintendent of the plant employing 103 men. He later went into newspaper work. He was feature writer on the *Springfield (Mass.) Homestead,* then the night man on the *Boston Globe,* and ultimately owned the *Chicopee Journal, Deerfield Valley Times* and *Caledonian-Record* in St. Johnsbury, VT. His extensive fiction writing for national magazines commenced when he worked for Governor Howe at the *Bennington Banner.*

Mr. Pelley was solicited by the sponsors of the Methodist Centenary Movement to go to the Orient on a layman's survey of foreign missionary work. When America joined other countries in the Siberian Intervention, he got into khaki in the Far East, becoming a Red Triangle man and impromptu consular carrier with the Allied troops in Siberia.

The Soviet Union was aflame with the assassination of the Royal Family and the murderous onslaught of the Bolshevists. The whole experience was soul chilling to Mr. Pelley and imbued him with the determination to prevent it happening in his own country.

In the early 1930s the "Silver Lodge" was built in Redmond, Washington and served as the meeting place for all the political and social activities of the *Silver Legion*, Mr. Pelley's national organization.

Members did all the work in constructing the building and maintaining it.

Here are some of the steadfast members of the *Silver Legion* who were present at most events at the *Lodge*. Many were part of the group that traveled with Mr. Pelley from San Diego to Seattle as members of the *"Cavalcade"* which promoted Mr. Pelley's bid for the presidency of the United States.

My brother, Walter, is on the far left of the top row. He rode freight trains all the way from Minnesota to Washington to be with Mr. Pelley and be part of his efforts.

Councils of Safety were organized locally in cities throughout the nation and held independent meetings supporting the national program. Their slogan was "For Christ and Constitution!"

They received literature from Headquarters and espoused the proposals of a "Christian Commonwealth" as presented by Mr. Pelley's book **No More Hunger**.

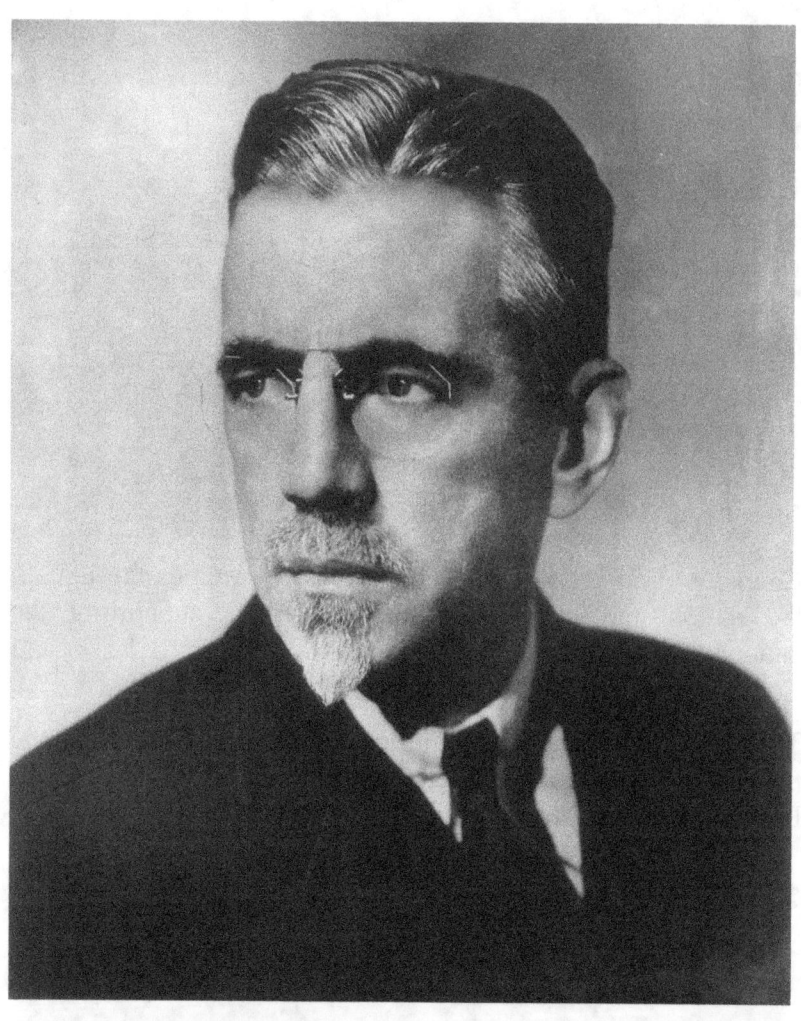

By the mid-1930s Mr. Pelley through his writings and activities had gotten considerable notoriety and he was being maligned and misrepresented to the public. This photo (incidentally very good in contrast to the others) appeared in the **Saturday Evening Post**. In the article, he was identified as one of the nation's "Star-Spangled Fascists."

A Federal Marshal escorts Mr. Pelley to the Federal Court in Indianapolis where he was to testify in his own behalf.

The trial of Mr. Pelley was held in this Federal building in Indianapolis, Indiana. On August 12, 1942 Judge Baltzell sentenced Mr. Pelley to fifteen years in a Federal penitentiary on the conviction of violating the wartime sedition law, the *1917 Espionage Act.*

Again, as on another occasion in history, a cry arose, "Crucify him, crucify him!" His accusers were jubilant, and the gullible cheered!

Three months later, shortly after Thanksgiving, I met Adelaide in this same building when she came down the same stairway that Charles Lindbergh, the "Lone Eagle," did after testifying in Mr. Pelley's behalf.

"We were meant for each other!"

Her Dad's philosophy is very compelling in noting that we all make pacts before we incarnate as to whom we will meet and what circumstances will enhance our spiritual awareness and sensitivity to all life.

These are nationally known defendants of the "Mass Sedition Trial" who were held in the Washington District Jail during their trial and later were freed of all charges.

While Mr. Pelley was detained in the Washington District Jail as a defendant in the Mass Sedition Trial, he was allowed to meet his first grandchild.

At that time, I had also been granted permission, along with Adelaide; to have 30-minute visits each month with her Dad. However, his attorney was able to have him brought to the "holding room" of the Federal Court where we had ample time to follow his instructions as to his planned legal actions.

On Valentine's Day, February 14, 1950, Mr. Pelley was granted parole after serving seven and a half years in prison. Resolution 170 introduced by Senator William Langer in the United States Congress demanding delayed justice for Mr. Pelley, along with thousands of letter by his supporters, brought about his release.

This is his first day home with Adelaide and me and his grandchildren.

Visitors from all over the country came to visit Mr. Pelley after he was home. Here is a small group from Florida who motored up to Indiana.

Included in the picture are Mrs. Pelley kneeling to the far left, several workers in the Plant, and Adelaide and me next to my brother, Edwin, on the top row.

Herma J. Jefferys, sitting here with Adelaide, was not only the youngest person, a graduate of Rollins College, to be hired by Mr. Pelley at his Asheville, NC Plant, but is at the present time (2008) the oldest remaining associate at the young age of 97.

She, Adelaide and I spearheaded and continued the work after Mr. Pelley died in 1965. Her lifetime loyalty and steadfastness will be remembered and blessed!

Mr. Pelley's love for all God's creatures extended itself to all life, including a special appreciation for the natural artistry of the Creator. He had a special fondness for dogs and all can remember his "Laska" who was with him when he experienced "My Seven Minutes in Eternity."

There were few times that dogs didn't occupy space at Soulcraft Headquarters.

A 16-millimeter movie camera was a constant companion to Mr. Pelley. His personal experience in Hollywood, and movies, made film an intrinsic element in his blood.

Hail but not Farewell!

Chapter Thirteen

Since when was this sedition?

Let us take a quick glance at portions of the indictment to learn what the government considered "sedition" in the Pelley Case in 1942. Bear in mind that the prosecution included in the indictment just those statements, extracted out of context, that they felt could be misconstrued to present a false over-all picture of Pelley's pro-American stand.

Later we will learn how evolving legal interpretations of the sedition acts, and particularly Supreme Court decisions, along with subsequent trials, underscores the constitutional right to question the acts of government during wartime. Expressions by those opposed to government policy during war were not seditious but "convictions" protected by the First Amendment guarantees of "freedom of the press" and "freedom of speech."

Legal scholars, including Professor Stone, concluded that Pelley would never have been convicted if such evolution of the sedition acts had occurred prior to his being indicted and tried in Indianapolis.

Consider the following quotations from the indictment itself and make your own judgment of the kind of "evidence" that was used against this courageous and fearless citizen to silence him. The prosecution extracted them largely from his magazine, *The Galilean,* and a brochure he wrote entitled "We fight for this Republic only!"

The prosecution waxed confident as they commenced reading the "evidence" but shortly found themselves unguardedly caught up in the patriotic substance of the passages.

Under the heading, "A platform for Real Patriotism," was extracted the following---

When a lot of fine, upstanding American lads are on the firing line abroad, battling for the Republic, and all they assume it represents, and a horde of incompetent, venal or queasy politicians are playing ducks and drakes with the war at home, using its opportunities to alter subtly our form of government, what course is the outraged but sagacious citizen to take?

In the first place, the United States should not have gotten into the war at all, for, aloof from it, and preserving a mighty neutrality, it rested secure in unchallengeable influence to shape the outcome from a dispassionate standpoint. Letting itself become a participant in actual hostilities, it lowered its proud position, sacrificed its prestige, and let itself descend into the caterwauling role of just another nation kicking into the stramash and obviously---the way that matters seem to be going after two months of it---playing second fiddle to Britain at that.

Under the heading "What America Should Do," the following appeared---

To rationalize that the United States got into the war because of an unprovoked attack on Pearl Harbor is fiddle-faddle. Unprovoked, indeed! All Americans are not fools . . .

They want their Administration to halt abruptly this unpatriotic and disastrous policy of stripping the ranks of our protective forces by shipping consignments of raw, half-trained recruits to aid strategizing Britain or soveitizing Russia on every battlefront on earth, call back all such forces wherever they may be located at present, and begin to put the American Republic in a condition of defense that can successfully withstand any sort of assault

84

that can conceivably be launched upon it for the next twenty year.

Under the heading "Why John Q. Public is Getting Angered," the following was taken---

Should a cynical citizenry root itself hoarse over such political carousel and agree that this Republic cannot win its war without it, or should hard Yankee common sense lay down a few ultimatums for a sweeping and drastic renovation, and consign the social nepotists to the trash-bins of oblivion? . . .

And they won't do it by destroying Government, either. They will do it by returning the nation to a Constitutionalism that scours. There's nothing wrong with our government or with our way of life or with our Republic itself but the internationalistic termites that have eaten their way into the country's staunch foundations.

Under the heading, "Minding Our Own Business," Pelley was quoted---

It is time to lay down the clearcut and unassailable policy that the United States has one concern, and one only: To apply its attention strictly to the continents that are North and South America, to get out of every other part of the world and stay out, to set up a Monroe Doctrine for the Western Hemisphere and stick to it, to ignore the Germans, the Russians, the British, the Chinese, the Japanese and the Martians, and apply itself concertedly to the business of fortifying and stabilizing American territory from Canada to Mexico and from Baltimore to San Francisco so that Christian Americans can live in reasonable welfare from now till doomsday without let or hindrance from any other power on the face of the globe.

85

When that policy is recognized and sincerely adhered to, nine tenths of the troubles of this Republic will vanish overnight.

Under the heading, "Construction in a Collapsing World," the following was included---

If we were honestly engaged in winning a war for the United States and none other, that would be one thing. But we are committed to winning a war for imperial Britain and Bolshevist Russia and China, which is something else again.

We do not propose to retreat on our own battlefronts a single inch, but when a situation is overdrawn, unnatural and predatory, in fields afar, and when we let ourselves be committed to a policy of expending billions today for foreign nations that by the overturn of a cabinet tomorrow may employ all that resources and equipment against us, we are not engaging in legitimate war but illegitimate gambling with our sovereignty as jackpot.

Is it conceivable by the wildest stretch of the imagination that such expressions could be construed as sedition? In the echo of such language, whence comes the accusation that Pelley was seeking to overthrow our form of government?

Doesn't the content and patriotic fervor of Mr. Pelley's words apply timely to an honest criticism and evaluation of our tragic war in Iraq?

Shouldn't such statements be the basic underpinnings of a true foreign policy regarding all nations?

Later, we will cover the Important Supreme Court decisions subsequent to his trial, and the legal thinking of a most important book, called "Perilous Times" which clearly exonerate Mr. Pelley.

Chapter Fourteen

The Mass Sedition Trial

MORE WAS YET to come. Much more. Roosevelt and the vested interests that thrive on war and human suffering were by no means content with their successful purge trial of Pelley in Indianapolis. Three months later, on Thanksgiving weekend, without warning even to his own family, Pelley was put in leg irons and suddenly moved from Terre Haute to Washington, D. C. to stand trial with 29 other critics in the notorious Mass Sedition Trial.

Those rounded up were writers, activists and publishers, all in varying degrees opposed to Communism and the war policies of the New Deal. Whereas Pelley had been convicted under the 1917 Sedition Law, otherwise known as the "wartime" act, the defendants in the Mass Trial were to be tried under the "peacetime" Smith Act that had been passed in 1940.

The prime point to be weighed here is that the wording of both sedition laws is almost verbatim; the charge of crime is substantially the same. In fact, the same evidence that was presented against Mr. Pelley in Indianapolis was now being presented against him in Washington.

What then of the constitutional prohibition that states, **nor shall any person be subject for the same offense to be twice put in jeopardy of his life or limb"?** Isn't it apparent that those determined to silence Mr. Pelley were trying to doubly assure themselves that his voice and pen would be muted?

Although the first indictment was returned on July 24, 1942, two other indictments had to be brought down before a third indictment on January 4, 1944 was considered sufficient to commence actual trial.

For eight months, starting on April 17, 1944, the prosecution vainly attempted to present a case. Out of 1100 documents, constituting some 18,000 pages, not a single piece of evidence had been introduced substantiating the charge when a mistrial was declared due to the sudden death of presiding Judge Eicher.

The prosecution was not able thereafter to bring the matter to trial despite the fact that over a million dollars of the taxpayers' money had been expended. Also, Chief Prosecutor O. John Rogge had made a trip to Germany in a futile attempt to find foreign evidence that would support his department's spurious charges.

On November 22, 1946, Chief Justice Bolitha J. Laws, of the U. S. District Court for the District of Columbia, dismissed the case in one of the most forceful decisions ever rendered from a Federal bench. He ruled:

> The case was called on September 20, 1946, for the purpose of setting a date for trial. On this occasion, Chief Prosecutor Rogge, being asked the third time in eight months the attitude of the prosecution, stated that there still remained in his mind the question whether there was sufficient evidence to meet the test of the Supreme Court cases. . . .

> If these defendants are guilty, it would seem that any serious doubt as to their guilt would be resolved in more than five years of intensive investigation by able counsel and investigators of the Department of Justice.

> But where it appears, as here, there is serious doubt as to the success of the case, and that the defendants, because of long delays granted over their objections, cannot obtain a fair trial, the court should exercise its discretion to deny prosecution. It would be both unjust and un-American to do otherwise. . . .

> Under the circumstances, to permit another trial, which conceivably would last more than a year, with new prosecutors and newly appointed counsel for defendants, with the eventual outcome in serious doubt, as Mr. Rogge

has stated to the Court on three occasions, would be a travesty on justice.

The very next day the noted columnist, Frank C. Waldrop, in a column headed "The Cheapest Act" in the **Washington Times Herald**, succinctly summarized the developments and ending of the infamous Mass Trial. He had this to say:

For disgrace and cheapness can you name anything by our great United States Government throughout its history to equal its performance in the so-called "sedition case"?

Chief Justice Bolitha J. Laws of the U. S. District Court here put the Department of Justice out of its misery yesterday by granting defense motions to dismiss the case. He said:

"In this circumstance, to permit another trial, which conceivably could last more than a year, with new prosecutors and newly appointed counsel for the defendants, with the eventual outcome in serious doubt . . . would be a travesty on justice"

That it would be, but no worse a travesty than the record to date. Except for the cold, official, provable facts of public record, anybody would be justified to thinking the whole story is a joke or a lie.

The Great Sedition Trial's history is sordid in every line. No single person who had a part in bringing it on can point with pride to an accomplishment of worth to grow out of it, for all the money it cost, for all the reputations it smeared or for all the unsuspecting American minds it poisoned.

The story begins, oh, we'll never know exactly all about that until the secret archives of the Department of Justice are broken open, as they should be, but for a formal date, put down July 1941.

That was when a special prosecutor for the Department of Justice, one William Power Maloney, went before a D. C. Grand Jury to allege some people had been violating the

Espionage Act of 1917, and the Alien Registration Act of 1940.

Maloney charged a conspiracy to violate the seditious propaganda sections of these acts. "Sedition" is the high crime of inciting resistance to the Government. It is just one slight step short of treason, which is giving open aid and comfort to an enemy.

Naturally, anybody accused of sedition any time is on a hot spot. Friends, avoid him. Acquaintances know him not. And given the state of public feeling in July 1941, all is multiplied.

Obviously, the United States Government and its special prosecutor, Mr. William Power Maloney, had upon them at that time a tremendous responsibility to protect innocent good names and observe common decency just as they had a tremendous responsibility to protect the nation from any internal enemies.

But what happened!

Well does this writer remember the day when some terrified lady members of the America First Committee were summoned to appear before the Grand Jury.

One was a Senator's wife. The others were private citizens. Against none could doubts of loyalty to the U. S. be raised by even the remotest suggestion. Their crime was that they were exercising their constitutional right to differ with the Administration in the great foreign policy debate then raging in America.

Still they felt Mr. Maloney's heavy hand upon their shoulders. So did many another. The Grand Jury proceedings were a scandal and an outrage. Secrets of the jury room leaked in a steady stream to Mr. Maloney's favored reporters, columnists and gossipmongers.

Well, finally an indictment was returned on July 24, 1942, and the real legal war began.

But for all his performance, Mr. Maloney's indictment was no good. In fact, the Department of Justice had to go back and do the whole thing over twice, so that not until January 4, 1944, was an indictment brought down that the Government cared to test in court.

Meanwhile, Mr. Maloney had been tested in court, also. The U. S. Supreme Court reversed his preliminary canter in the field with language that would blister the hide of a rhinoceros.

That was on March 1, 1943, in the matter of George Sylvester Viereck, a German agent convicted of improperly registering with the State Department.

Maloney had prosecuted Viereck in a warm-up for the main event of the sedition trial. The Supreme Court reversed the conviction, 5 to 2, on the ground that Viereck was being tried for acts committed before the law was passed under which he was accused.

In the course of the reversal, the late Harlan F. Stone, then Chief Justice of the Supreme Court, had this to say of Maloney:

"He indulged in an appeal wholly irrelevant to any facts or issues of the case, the purpose and effect of which could only have been to arouse passion and prejudice.

At a time when passion and prejudice are heightened by emotions stirred by our participation in a great war, we do not doubt that the remarks addressed to the jury were highly prejudicial and that they were offensive to the dignity and good order in which all proceedings in court should be conducted . . ."

Only once before in its history had the Supreme Court ever so directly and fiercely reprimanded an attorney and never before had it ever felt the need to do so with a United States prosecutor.

That was nothing, however, to what followed.

The third indictment came on for trial April 19, 1944, with 30 defendants. For eight months it ground away getting nowhere and ended in a mistrial when the presiding judge dropped dead. The Government has not dared since to do anything positive about it one way or the other.

Two of the defendants have died, also, and O. John Rogge, the special prosecutor who succeeded Maloney, has been fired by the Department of Justice for shooting off his mouth.

There just was no luck in that case for anybody. And why? Because it was a case bred in malice, prosecuted in hate, and pursued in bigotry. It had purposes far wider than the mere trial of people accused of a crime. It was a disgrace to America.

There isn't much that can be added to the caustic summation that Mr. Waldorf made of the Trial and its outcome.

The final curtain had come down on the judicial sham and political persecution called the Mass Sedition Trial!

Chapter Fifteen

Important Supreme Court decisions

THREE important Supreme Court decisions came down that clarified what was necessary to sustain the charge of sedition. They were the singular decisions that led Chief Justice Laws to dismiss the Mass Sedition Trial because the prosecution admitted that a conviction could not be sustained in light of them.

Hartzell vs. United States (322 U. S. 680) stands out irrefutably as it dealt with the same sections 33 and 34 of Title 50 of the U. S. Code under which Pelley was convicted. In this decision the Supreme Court ruled and held that a conviction under the law was illegal unless two elements were made to affirmatively appear from the court transcript and record, these being:

> **A subjective element, consisting of specific intent or evil purpose at the time the allegedly criminal acts were committed, to cause insubordination or disloyalty in the armed forces, or to obstruct the recruiting and enlistment service; and**

> **An objective element, consisting in a clear and present danger that the activities alleged to be criminal will bring about the evils described under the subjective element.**

Nowhere in the transcript or record of the Pelley case in Indiana can there be found one shred of evidence permitting of a finding that the subjective and objective elements mentioned in the Hartzell case were proved beyond a reasonable doubt.

In his book, **Perilous Times,** Geoffrey Stone refers to the Hartzell Case and underscores that Pelley would not have been convicted if the Supreme Court decision, along with other cases, had preceded the Indianapolis trial.

Baumgartner vs. United States (322 U. S. 665) the Supreme Court in concerning itself with the right of a citizen to free speech critical of our institutions and leadership, said in part:

> **One of the prerogatives of American citizenship is the right to criticize public men and measures, and that means not only informed and responsible criticism but the freedom to speak foolishly and without moderation. . . It would be foolish to deny that even blatant intolerance toward some of the presupposition of the democratic faith may not imply rooted disbelief in our system of government.**

This important decision by the Supreme Court simply underscored Pelley's right to free speech and free press, and that spoken or written words, in and of themselves, do not constitute the crime---there must also be proved beyond a reasonable doubt the subjective and objective elements in the Hartzell case, else there is no crime.

Geoffrey Stone in his book, **Perilous Times,** cites how a new legal perspective emerged since the passing of the 1917 Espionage Act which underscored the constitutional right of a citizen to be both aggressively and caustically critical of the actions and policies of incumbent government, particularly during war, without being guilty of "sedition."

Vierick vs. United States (318 U. S. 236) in which the Supreme Court reversed a lower court conviction because of the inflammatory and prejudicial argument resorted to by government counsel. In the closing argument of the Pelley trial one of the associate counsel for the government described Pelley as "the arch-Quisling of America," as a "Benedict Arnold," as an "Aaron Burr," as "the blackest type of murderer." as "Hitler's American fuehrer," and exhorted the jury to convict Pelley, "in order to preserve the safety of the country."

Concerning this type of prosecution, the Supreme Court stated the following:

At a time when passion and prejudice are heightened by emotions stirred by our participation in a great war, we do not doubt that those remarks addressed to the jury were highly prejudicial, and that they were offensive to the dignity and good order with which all proceedings in court should be conducted. We think that the trial judge should have stopped counsel's discourse without waiting for an objection.

The United States Attorney is the representative not of an ordinary party to a controversy, but of a sovereignty whose obligation to govern impartially is as compelling as its obligation to govern at all; and whose interest, therefore, in a criminal prosecution is not that it shall win a case, but that justice shall be done.

These monumental Supreme Court decisions came down subsequent to Pelley's Indiana conviction. They overwhelmingly bore out that his conviction was contrary to due process of law, that he did not have a fair trial under constitutional guarantees and that there had been a substantial and egregious miscarriage of justice. With the highest court in the land declaring in his favor, it seemed but a matter of legal routine for Pelley to receive his much belated freedom.

On October 15, 1946 Pelley's able Washington counsel filed in the Indianapolis Federal Court a Petition for a *Writ of Error Coram Nobis,* which embodied the forgoing Supreme Court decisions upon which the Mass Sedition Trial was dismissed. The United States Attorney, B. Howard Caughram, resisted it solely on the grounds that the Indianapolis court lacked jurisdiction. Therefore, on December 9, 1946, a petition for leave to file a *Writ of Coram Nobis* was made to the Circuit Court of Appeals in Chicago. Ten days later the Circuit Court of Appeals denied the petition.

This first attempt by Pelley to get relief was denied without any substantial review of the Indianapolis conviction or relevant consideration of the Supreme Court decisions. Perhaps B.

Howard Caughran, who sat briefly on the bandwagon of the national original trial, advanced this amazing logic to the Pelley petition.

> **If petitioner is entitled to the relief prayed because of the decision in the Hartzell case, then every other defendant who was convicted of a violation of Section 33 and 34 of Title 30 of the United States Code before the decision of the Hartzell case, which followed the decisions of the Supreme Court announced up to that time, would now likewise be entitled to file a motion for a _Writ of Coram Nobis._**

> **It would be unreasonable to expect the district courts of the United States to reopen all judgments entered by them in conformity with the law as interpreted by said district courts in the light of the decisions handed down by the Supreme Court before the decision in the Hartzell case in June of 1944. Such procedure would result in confusion and chaos in the administration of justice in the Federal courts.**

Never was a more stupefying declaration made by an officer of so-called justice in the interests of public probity. A Federal prosecutor acting under the authority for and under the authority of the Justice Department, had the temerity to declare in substance: We concede that under recent decisions of the Supreme Court the man is probably serving a long-term sentence in the penitentiary illegally, but it would cause too much confusion (loss of face) for the Department of Justice to correct the matter, so we oppose any court action to liberate him.

Keep the man in jail then, to save the Department of Justice and the Federal courts from "confusion and chaos"! But this was only the beginning of a new phase of illegal maneuvering and subterfuge to be resorted to by the Justice Department and concurred in by the courts. Powerful influences in and behind the Roosevelt Administration were determined to perpetuate Pelley's illegal imprisonment irrespective of the flagrant denial of his most sacred constitutional rights.

Chapter Sixteen

Writart of Habeas Corpus Suspended!

O<small>N</small> JANUARY 7, 1947 a *Petition for a Writ of Habeas Corpus* was filed with the Indianapolis Court since this was the court of original trial. Immediately representatives of the Justice Department resisted the *Petition* on the grounds that Pelley was physically held in Washington and therefore the Indianapolis court lacked jurisdiction to hear the merits of the petition. Judge Bultzell concurred.

In view of this ruling, attorneys for Pelley on January 13, 1947, filed a Petition for a *Writ of Habeas Corpus* with the District Court of the U. S. for the District of Columbia within whose jurisdiction Pelley was being physically held pending appeals on the Mass Sedition dismissal. Unabashedly, representatives of the Justice Department now contended that the Washington court didn't have jurisdiction.

They were blind to the indisputable circumstance that either the Indianapolis or the Washington court had to have jurisdiction to entertain the merits of the petition!

Whereas they had contended that the Indianapolis court didn't have jurisdiction of Pelley because he was physically in Washington, they now contended that although Pelley was in Washington, the Washington court didn't have jurisdiction because he was there only technically, by a court order *Habeas Corpus ad Prosequendum.*

Inconceivably, Judge Goldsborough concurred with the Department.

For Pelley, sitting behind steel doors and iron bars, Judge Goldsborough's ruling meant one thing only: Representatives of the Department of Justice had succeeded in blocking all access to the courts and thereby had suspended the *Writ of*

Habeas Corpus despite the specific guarantees of the Constitution that it shall not be suspended!

Upon the advice of our legal counsel I approached the Justice Department seeking a stipulation that determined jurisdiction, which would permit my father-in-law to have one of the courts hear the merits of his *Petition*. The Department of Justice must certainly agree to one of the courts having jurisdiction.

Arrogantly, I was informed, "We are resorting to dilatory tactics and we'll resort to all the damn dilatory tactics we want to!" I was equally adamant in replying, "You are consistent with all your past delaying tactics and are blatantly ignoring the admonition of the Supreme Court which stated "the Department's main interest is not that it shall win a case, but that justice shall be done."

Openly and contemptuously, members of the Justice Department were deliberately engaged in circumventing the Constitution itself!

On June 30, 1947 the Court of Appeals for the District of Columbia upheld Judge Goldsborough's ruling. Only the Supreme Court of the United States now remained. While Pelley was awaiting a ruling by the High Court, John O'Donnell, outstanding political columnist for both the **Times Herald** in Washington and the New York **Daily News** had this to say in his column of October 2, 1947:

> **Next Monday the nine members of the Supreme Court of the United States will be returned from their working vacations and must make up their judicial minds about the most important issue which has disturbed the judicial branch of the United States since the Civil War days when Lincoln and Chief Justice Taney tangled over who was top guy---the Chief Justice of the United States or the Chief Executive in the White House.**
>
> **What the boys must decide is whether William Dudley Pelley, the most important American publisher tossed into**

the can for "sedition" by direct orders of the late Franklin Roosevelt, is in fact a "political prisoner" and whether in cold legal fact this Republic of ours is going through the ancient French double-crossing judicial trickery which made the Dreyfus case one for the books.

A sound and experienced reporter, Mr. Phillip Warden of the Washington bureau of the Chicago Tribune, has blown a loud and commanding whistle which promptly calls attention to the politically slick and, at heart, cowardly trickiness with which the boys are ducking the punches and haven't the honest decency to go to make for a final showdown.

Mr. Warden reports that members of Congress are now going into action in the Pelley case and raises the important question: Why should Pelley, eligible for parole, be held in the can when mobsters of the Capone era, probably with political pull, can get quick action from the Department of Justice and White House

REPORTS reporter Warden:

"Pelley was sentenced to 15 years in prison after his conviction by a federal court jury in Indianapolis, 1942, and sent to the federal penitentiary at Terre Haute, Indiana.

"Attorney T. Emmett McKenzie of Washington, said he is seeking an inquiry to determine why the parole board, which speeded the release of four Chicago hoodlums in an action which resulted in a Congressional investigation, has refused to act in Pelley's case.

"McKenzie said Senators Corden (R) of Oregon, McCarthy (R) of Wisconsin, Capehart (R) of Indiana, Revercomb (R) of West Virginia, Capper (R) of Kansas, and Hawkes (R) of New Jersey, and Representative Rankin (D) of Mississippi are among numerous members of Congress who have written to the parole board.

"McKenzie said that Pelley was eligible for parole on August 12, 1947. Because Pelley has been held in the

District of Columbia city jail since being brought here from Terre Haute as a defendant in the recently dismissed mass sedition trial and is not in a federal prison, the parole board for weeks refused to consider his application, McKenzie said.

"McKenzie said this barrier was overcome this week but now the board is refusing to hear Pelley's application on the ground that Pelley is seeking a *writ of habeas corpus* and as long as he is in court on this matter, the parole board has no right to parole him.

"I am inquiring to determine how it could happen that four people in Chicago (the four former Capone gangsters paroled recently under mysterious circumstances after serving only brief portions of their sentences) had their applications for parole so greatly facilitated when with respect to Pelley, I find that although he is eligible for consideration, this same board declines to even consider his case," McKenzie said.

"MCKENZIE said that since Pelley's conviction in 1942 he has learned of the existence of documentary evidence which he believes will prove his contention that Pelley was innocent of the charges made against him.

"Pelley was convicted for being anti-Semitic, not for sedition as the court records show, McKenzie charged during the interview.

"McKenzie revealed that he was making this same charge in his appeal to the Supreme Court of the United States for a writ of certiorari. McKenzie is seeking to have the Supreme Court hear him on his contention that the federal court of the District of Columbia has jurisdiction over Pelley and is required to grant Pelley's application for a *writ of habeas corpus.*

The local federal judges have refused to accept jurisdiction over Pelley, claiming he is under the jurisdiction of the Indianapolis court, which sentenced him to prison. The Indianapolis court claimed Pelley was in Washington,

100

where he was taken for the sedition trial, and the Washington court had jurisdiction over him."

Answers to both O'Donnell's inquiry and Pelley's status came down from the Supreme Court on October 27, 1947. The high court denied the *Writ of Certiorari,* thus refusing even to consider the constitutional question of jurisdiction for a *Writ of Habeas Corpus.*

Immediately a petition for a re-hearing on the *Writ of Certiorari* was filed. Again, a summary denial.

Congressional Investigation Sought

ONE need not be a Doctor of Laws from an ivy-covered college to recognize the alarming implications for all citizens when the *Writ of Habeas Corpus* can be arbitrarily suspended. For this is the most sacred constitutional right all citizens possess against oppressive government. Because of its importance, the Founding Fathers made it part of the Constitution itself.

Article 1, Section 9, Clause 2, of the Constitution reads as follows: **The privilege of the Writ of Habeas Corpus shall not be suspended, unless when in cases of rebellion or invasion the public safety may require it!**

In Pelley's case where both the Judicial and Executive Branches of government were involved in denying a citizen access to the courts and thereby suspending the *Writ of Habeas Corpus,* the threat to constitutional government exceeded the mere stage of alarm. It was stark reality!

For Pelley there remained only one course of action. Should not the circumstance of his illegal confinement through suspension of the *Writ of Habeas Corpus,* command Congressional investigation? Certainly, both the House and Senate Judiciary Committees should have been compelled to consider the question: Can the Department of Justice, prosecuting in the name of the United States, make such arrangement for the penal confinement of a citizen of the United States as to suspend the *Writ of Habeas Corpus* for such citizen?

Here, again, Adelaide played a persistent and diligent role in rallying citizens across the land to the flagrant unconstitutional treatment of her father. Thousands of concerned citizens signed petitions and wrote letters pleading for a Congressional investigation of the Pelley injustice. They recognized that Pelley was now a martyr to New Deal rancor's and directly contacted members of Congress.

Adelaide underscored that what they were doing to her father **could be done to each and every citizen**.

The reaction of Congress was disconcerting. The whole effort was to no avail. It is one thing when political appointees to both the Justice Department and the Federal Courts display criminal negligence respecting the rights of an individual citizen. It is something much more serious when a people's elected representatives evince more concern about getting re-elected than they do in supporting and defending the Constitution.

As one United States Senator put it, "There is no question of the flagrant wrong done Mr. Pelley, but politically he is just too "hot a potato" to handle!"

With two refusals by the Supreme Court to determine the question of jurisdiction, and with the Congress of the United States refusing to intercede in his behalf, a whole year elapsed for Pelley during which time he was without any court in the entire land that would entertain his *Writ of Habeas Corpus* pleading. He had recourse to no action whatsoever leading toward relief from illegal confinement.

Chapter Seventeen

Pelley Returned to Indiana

ON December 20, 1947, with the Mass Sedition case passed completely into history, the Bureau of Prisons returned Pelley to the Federal penitentiary at Terre Haute, Indiana. The Indiana court now accepted jurisdiction and a *Petition for a Writ of habeas Corpus* was filed.

On May 25, 1948 the *Petition* was dismissed without a hearing of any kind. There was no consideration of the merits. There was no judicial determination of Pelley's original conviction in light of the important Supreme Court decisions that had come down after his trial in Indianapolis. Appeal met with the same evasive fate.

A number of further pleadings were filed after Pelley was returned to Indiana but their listing here would add little but repetition in supporting the already over- whelming denial of due process of law accorded Pelley.

In each and every pleading both the District and Appeals courts dismissed the actions without a fair hearing or consideration of the facts or the law. It was simply contended, as did Judge Steckler in Indianapolis, that the "matter has been completely adjudicated and there is nothing to be considered."

Although Pelley had become eligible for parole on August 12, 1947, having served one-third of his fifteen-year sentence, it wasn't until February 14, 1950 that he was finally released on parole. Again, it was evident that there was one law for Pelley and another law for others, including habitual gangsters who were released immediately upon serving one-third of their sentences!

Only after a number of Mandamus actions had been filed in the Federal Courts seeking a judicial ruling that the Parole Board abide by the provisions of the Parole Act, only after Senator

William Langer introduced Senate Resolution 170 calling for a full and complete investigation of the Parole Board, only after thousands of letters were directed to members of Congress, was parole obtained for Pelley!

Whereas Pelley was released on Valentine's Day, 1950, it wasn't until August 12, 1957 that he was free from the restrictions of parole. Few people were aware that during the seven and a half years he was on parole the Parole Board could at any time arbitrarily rule that even such restricted freedom was not "compatible with society" and he could be returned to durance vile.

Even more of a threat was the fact that in such event he would have to commence his 15-year sentence all over again from the beginning. To those who unknowingly questioned why Pelley didn't come out swinging, it should be added that one of the provisions of parole was that he could not engage in political activities of any nature.

Too often Pelley's patriotic critics were those who had gone into hiding when Pelley continued to stand forth and proclaim the truth as he saw it, irrespective of consequences to his person.

The consequences, or "The Price of Truth," are the brief, documented story you hole in your hands.

I want to conclude the foregoing coverage of William Dudley Pelley as the Twentieth Century's most outstanding political prisoner, and most outstanding crusader for peace with economic justice, with a most poignant and encompassing piece written by his legal counsel, T. Emmett McKenzie.

It encompasses and encapsulates the pertinent thinking of Charles A. Beard, the nation's outstanding historian, Professor Geoffrey R. Stone, Dean of the University of Chicago Law School, and leading members of Congress all within the framework of the Constitution and the specific laws relevant to "Sedition."

Mr. McKenzie's summation is a classic, which should be paramount when, and wherever, the Pelley Case is being considered.

Chapter Eighteen

Vengeance Under the Law!

IT IS JANUARY 1941.

Two men whose convictions and principles have already decided their ultimate fate face the future.

One is Franklin Delano Roosevelt in whose name scores of thousands shall be consigned to death, lunacy, and lingering agony, those being the common people, the people to be drafted, to be thrown into battle, to be shuffled about as checkers upon the board of destiny.

With Roosevelt other thousands who are to become the darlings of our time---these being the friends of the War Administration---the people who are to obtain the war contracts for munitions of war, the special privileges that attend high civilian position, position where no shells thunder and no bayonets tear out the innards.

The other man is William Dudley Pelley in whose name none are to suffer or die. In whose name there is to be waged a desperate but losing battle to keep our Nation out of World War II. In whose name the sacred guarantee of Amendment I to the Constitution of the United States---that dealing with the Right of Free Speech; and Amendment V to the Constitution of the United States---that dealing with the Right to a Fair Trial under Due Process of Law, are to be wantonly and maliciously read out of the Constitution and our Way of Life.

The votes of November 1940 have been tabulated and once again Franklin Delano Roosevelt has become President of the United States.

In Europe and Asia the fires and carnage of ruthless war are devouring civilization and ravishing the liberties of man---the being created in the Image of the Lord.

107

In America there is Peace!

In the White House President Roosevelt contemplates his rendezvous with destiny, and the fate of millions who shall live, die, hunger, bleed and suffer helplessly, awaits his public commitment of the power, force and resources of the United States of America.

Shortly, our newly re-elected President will hurl us into the horrendous maelstrom of global warfare, and what we have hitherto known as the "American Way of Life" shall be no more.

Concerning peace, President Roosevelt proclaimed at Philadelphia, October 23, 1940, that a Republican charge that the Roosevelt "administration wishes to lead this country into war", was a base calumny and a deliberate lie.

On October 30, 1940, at Boston, Candidate Roosevelt promised, "I have said this before, but I shall say it again and again and again: Your boys are not going to be sent into any foreign wars."

On November 2, 1940, Candidate Roosevelt vowed, "Your President says this country is not going to war."

These, his promises, were explicit but the conduct of the promiser had already stigmatized Roosevelt promises as having a counterfeit ring.

True, the words of the several promises were easy of comprehension; but the devious working of the minds that made the promises was known to be more cunning than frank---and the promises were suspect. The people has an uneasy feeling that the language had been employed more to conceal than to reveal the real purpose of the speaker.

Notwithstanding the oft-repeated Roosevelt pledges, the heavy and constant threat of marching to a foreign war, which was none of our concern, oppressed millions of our citizens. The parents, wives and children of our young American manhood vaguely but persistently struggled with an impending sense of doom.

Earlier a Gallop Poll had revealed that 83 percent of our populace was opposed to participation in a foreign war, but the 83 percent were horribly fearful their desires for peace would come to naught.

How right they were!

Mostly they were inarticulate. Fear, anxiety and apprehension for their personal liberties and for the safety of their loved ones they had in full, helpless measure. Of "what to do about it" they had solely and only a hopeful, childlike faith and trust in the promise of the Man in the White House.

Faith and trust in a promise which led not to the much desired and fervently hoped for peace, but to Roosevelt's passionately sought and hotly pursued bloody, flaming Armageddon. A promise which contrary to its plain terms, scourged us into another war to end all wars, to insure democracy, and to guarantee the rights of minorities, in our lifetime.

A war, which still rages. A war, which has brought no peace. A war which finds not only the destiny of this nation, but the very privilege of living and breathing dependent upon which shall first resort to atomic warfare, bacteriological warfare or warfare of a nature so utterly hideous and repulsive that the warmakers dare not disclose its nature and operation.

Thus for the Roosevelt promise, and so for its fulfillment.

Nonetheless, patriots whose love for this country and for its God-given freedom burned brightly, sought desperately to save and to keep the peace, to conserve our manpower, our unmatched liberties and our national honor.

Men who knew not only the words and the music to "My Country 'Tis of Thee", but likewise the sacred meaning of that glorious hymn, were determined that no renewal of the endless feuds and wars of decadent Europe should serve again to plunge this nation into the holocaust of international war.

Foremost in this gallant group was one William Dudley Pelley, the Massachusetts-born son of a Methodist clergyman. A true citizen of the United States whose British-Irish lineage quickly grasped and fiercely maintained those principles of Liberty, Justice and Democracy he had come to know and love within the shadows of Plymouth Rock, Bunker Hill and the myriad New England shrines of the American Revolution.

Not one to quibble or equivocate Pelley early and late decried the foreign policy of the war-bent administration. Boldly, fearlessly and frankly he warned in season and out that the policies of the Roosevelt Administration must inevitably and inexorably lead us into the raging global warfare.

With equal candor and vigor he charged our foreign policy would eventually play into the hands of Russia, and strengthen the Communistic design for world rebellion.

That it would, beyond doubt, force and compel either Germany or Japan or both to make an ultimate attack upon us; and when to the great act of war, Pelley boldly castigated the administration for the scheming and conniving that had resulted in Japan's decisive action.

Pelley was not alone at this time.

Mindful that 83 percent of our people were totally opposed to involvement in the war, statesmen in both Houses of Congress openly and vigorously expressed their opposition to the administration's foreign policy.

During the debate on the Lend-Lease Bill the following branded the Act as a war measure:

Representatives: Thomas A. Jenkins, Ohio; Bartel Jonkman, Michigan; Usher Burdick, N. Dakota; Hugh Peterson, Georgia; James O'Connor, Montana; Melvin Hass, Minnesota; Martin Sweeney, Ohio; Dewey Short, Missouri; Clifford Hope,

Kansas; Phillip Bennett, Missouri; George Tinkham, Massachusetts; H. Carl Anderson, Minnesota; Gerald Landis, Indiana.

Senators: Bennett Clark, Missouri; Pat McCarran, Nevada; Burton K. Wheeler, Montana; David I. Walsh, Massachusetts; Arthur Vandenberg, Michigan; Wayland C. Brooks, Illinois; Robert M. LaFollette, Wisconsin; Robert A. Taft, Ohio.

The later Administration Bill to amend the Neutrality Act to authorize the arming of United States merchant ships at a time when this country was not at war, was branded as a war bill by the following:

Representatives: George H. Tinkham, Massachusetts; Daniel Reed, New York; Harold Knutson, Minnesota; John M. Coffee, Washington; John M. Robison, Kentucky; George W. Gillie, Indiana; H. Carl Anderson, Minnesota.

Senators: Arthur Vandenberg, Michigan; Gerald Nye, N. Dakota; Robert M. LaFallette, Wisconsin; Wayland C. Brooks, Illinois; D. Worth Clark, Idaho; David Walsh, Massachusetts; Burton K. Wheeler, Montana.

Confronted by such opposition a citizen who truly believed in Democracy, who believed in the rights of majorities, might well pause and consider the wisdom of his program. But Roosevelt was no such person. The mind that had conceived the Supreme Court Packing Plan and the "Purge" of his own party members lacking in desired docility was not now disposed to act in the democratic tradition.

Opposed, openly and logically by renowned leaders of both political parties, and by the great majority of all the people, Roosevelt reacted in typical dictatorial manner and personally assumed command of the smear brigade. Addressing the Governing Board of the Pan-American Union at the White House, the President stated on May 27, 1941:

There is, of course, a small group of sincere, patriotic men and women whose real passion for peace has shut their eyes to the ugly realities of international banditry and to the need to resist it at all costs. I am sure they are embarrassed by the sinister support they are receiving from the enemies of democracy in our midst, the Bundists, and Fascists, and Communists, and every group devoted to bigotry and racial and religious intolerance.

It is no mere coincidence that all the arguments put forward by these enemies of democracy, all their attempts to confuse and divide our people and to destroy public confidence in our Government, all their defeatist forebodings that Britain and democracy are already beaten, all their selfish promises that we can "do business" with Hitler, all of these are but echoes of the words that have been poured out from the Axis bureaus of propaganda.. These same words have been used before in other countries, to scare them, to divide them, to soften them up. Invariably, those same words have formed the advance guard of physical attack.

Withal Mr. Pelley had yet to learn the bitter fact, that address embodied his impending doom. He was opposed to war, Roosevelt was for war, and all who stood in opposition to the Roosevelt war program were enemies of Democracy. Strangely enough, as the address shows, Russians and communists were then allied with Hitler. Some little time later they were to abandon Hitler and to become allied with us, and then the real enemies of democracy, the communists, became over night our beloved brothers, crusaders for liberty and democracy.

And strangely enough with the passage of a bit more time they were to again turn against us; and this very day in the summer of 1948, they actively menace and threaten the safety and continued existence of this Republic.

Another Roosevelt heritage!

True enough, then as now, Amendment I to the Constitution of the United States provided amongst other things that: Congress shall make no law . . . abridging the freedom of speech, or of the press . . . a legal principle well-known to Mr. Pelley.

But Mr. Pelley was not menaced by any Act of Congress. He was being singled out by a President whose contempt for Congress has been long known, and whose determination to efface effective opposition was soon to become known.

Mr. Pelley was to shortly discover that while United States Senators and Members of Representatives, publishers of great metropolitan daily newspapers, communists in good standing with "Good Old Joe" and certain radical leaders of communistic inspired unions might openly and publicly buck into the Roosevelt war program, at the cost of no more than a Roosevelt scolding, the price to him was to be Life Imprisonment!

Fifty-two years of age, without great wealth, and lacking powerful political influence, Pelley stood revealed to the war administration as a perfect "victim". An ideal target against which to hurl the entire might, power and authority of the great United States of America, to the end that by making an "example" of him, the silence of all others of ordinary stature would be most certainly compelled.

Did there come a time in your community when unfavorable criticism of Roosevelt and his policies suddenly become dangerous?

When ugly rumors spread about concerning certain citizens who after loudly and publicly complaining of the war administration suddenly found federal investigations prying into their private lives?

When we had in this country the vague, shadowy fear hitherto known only in foreign lands dominated by foreign police?

That was but one attack upon our liberties, the over-all plan envisaged much more.

War!

Regimentation!

Government control over everything, be it merchandising, publish, publishing, broadcasting, laboring or farming.

The creation of a gigantic bureaucracy in Washington, consecrated to the communistic ideal of making the State, God and the people the abject slaves, with tens of thousands of intricate rules, regulations, forms, charts and reports covering man's every move from the cradle to the grave.

With a host of investigators descending upon the people to pry into their books, their businesses, their factories, their very home, and a ready jail awaiting any and all who failed, refused or neglected to play the game.

These were the things, which William Dudley Pelley wisely foreseeing set out to oppose and prevent when he cast his lot with 83 percent who desired no war.

And who will now say that he was wrong?

That the war has brought anything good to this country or to its citizens?

That the illimitable resources of blood, suffering, human wreckage, dead youth, money, munitions and resources were wisely spent to gain the grim and menacing position we occupy in the world of today?

In June, 1942, a Grand Jury, sitting in Indianapolis, Indiana, returned an indictment charging William Dudley Pelley with the offense of "Sedition".

The document consists of 62 pages of single-space close printing.

It is signed by B. Howard Caughran, United States Attorney, at Indianapolis, Indiana.

By Oscar R. Ewing, Special Assistant to the Attorney to the Attorney General at Washington, D. C.

By Henry A. Schweinhaut, Special Assistant to the Attorney General at Washington, D. C.

United States Attorney Caughran was a necessary party to the indictment; in his District he was supposed to prosecute in the name of the United States of America.

His status in the government has not changed. He remains and continues in the same position, a figure-head.

Special Assistant Oscar Ewing advanced rapidly after the Pelley Case. Today he is Administrator of the Federal Security Agency, which consists of: Food and Drug Administration, Office of Education, Office of Vocational Rehabilitation, Public Health Service (including Freedmen's Hospital), Social Security Administration, Bureau of Employer's Compensation, Employees' Compensation Appeals Board, and St. Elizabeth's Hospital.

Special Assistant Henry A. Schweinhaut has likewise experienced the good will of the Administration, which prosecuted Pelley. Today he is an Associate Justice of the District Court of the United States for the District of Columbia.

William Dudley Pelley has experienced the crushing vengeance of the same Administration, and today he languishes in the United States Reformatory at Terre Haute, Indiana, having been on August 12, 1942, sentenced to a term of 15 years imprisonment for the offense of "sedition".

What, to you, is Sedition?

Do you find it easy of definition and explanation, or is it difficult to define and explain? Is it the type and kind of alleged offense which need not mean anything in particular, and which may embrace almost anything?

Lexicographers generally define it as an insurrectionary act.

William Dudley Pelley was charged with Sedition because he had stated Franklin D. Roosevelt desired to involve this country into World War II.

Is that insurrection or is it the truth?

William Dudley Pelley was charged with Sedition because he had stated the foreign policy of Franklin D. Roosevelt was planned and designed to involve us either with Japan or Germany.

Is that insurrection or is it the truth?

William Dudley Pelley was charged with Sedition because he had stated the foreign policy goaded Japan into making an attack upon us, and that we had ample reason to suspect the time, place and manner of their attack.

Is that insurrection or is it the truth?

William Dudley Pelley was charged with Sedition because he had stated the Roosevelt foreign policy would eventually bankrupt us.

Is that insurrection or is it the truth?

William Dudley Pelley was charged with Sedition because he had stated we had provoked the attack upon the Philippines, which we were hopelessly unable to repel.

Is that insurrection or is it the truth?

William Dudley Pelley was charged with Sedition because he had stated we were not prepared for war that our armament, as of early 1941, was "on order".

Is that insurrection or is it the truth?

William Dudley Pelley was charged with Sedition because he had stated our gifts, loan and grants of ships, aircraft and munitions to England had weakened our military position.

Is that insurrection or is it the truth?

116

William Dudley Pelley was charged with Sedition because he had opposed our temporary union with communistic Russia, and had prophesied the adventure would ultimately bring us bitter fruit indeed.

Is that insurrection or is it the truth?

And if a citizen of this Republic, not the slave or the serf of a foreign dictatorship, foresees that the policy of our elected President is inevitably bound to bring us to death, debt and destruction, is it Sedition to cry out against that policy?

Is it a crime for the citizen of the United States to criticize the Administration in power?

Is free speech the right to speak freely and as vigorously as one pleases, or is it a right limited and circumscribed by the whims and caprices of whomsoever happens to occupy the White House?

In Baumgartner v United States, 322 United States Reports, p. 665, the Supreme Court of the United states said:

One of the prerogatives of American Citizenship is the right to criticize public men and measures, and that means not only informed and responsible criticism but the freedom to speak foolishly and without moderation.

So, eventually the 62-page indictment becomes of relative unimportance.

The important proposition is:

May a citizen be legally jailed for life because he not only disagrees with the policy of the administration but further undertakes to oppose it and substitute another democratic policy which has for its keystone the advancement of THIS COUNTRY, FIRST; the well-being of OUR PEOPLE, FIRST!

T. Emmett McKenzie

Counsel for William Dudley Pelley

Chapter Nineteen

"Perilous Times"

Some sixty years after Mr. Pelley's conviction credible public confirmation appeared exonerating him. Adelaide and I were elated and felt extreme satisfaction that the soundness of our efforts to vindicate her father's courageous position had been vouched for publicly.

Such vindication was the appearance (2004) of a book called **Perilous Times** by Geoffrey R. Stone. The subtitle to Mr. Stone's book states, "Free Speech in Wartime, From the Sedition Act of 1798 to the War on Terrorism." Mr. Stone is someone other than a newspaper reporter or political personality. He is a legal scholar with outstanding credentials.

On the flap of the book is stated: "Geoffrey E. Stone, the Harry Kalven, Jr. Distinguished Service Professor of Law at the University of Chicago, was dean of the law school from 1987 to 1994 and provost of the University from 1994 to 2002. He recently represented Fred Korematsu in an *amicus curiae* brief in the Supreme Court of the United States in the Quantanamo Bay case."

We, of course, were personally gratified with Mr. Stone's singling out Mr. Pelley as the primary victim of political vindictiveness and injustice during WWII. Our only regret is that he did echo some of the unfounded characterizations such as "Pelley founded the Silver Legion of America, an organization dedicated to the bringing of fascism to the United States."

It was obvious that he was not familiar with the proposals of **No More Hunger** in which Mr. Pelley outlined a democratic society with the widest dispersal of political and economic power to the people with full implementation of equal human

119

rights. Its proposals are the very antithesis of fascism in which government despotically controls the economic and political life of the people with brutal suppression of all opposition.

However, Mr. Stone does a precise and thorough job of underscoring the legal background of "sedition" and how Mr. Pelley was wrongly convicted. His book should be fully read to appreciate the consistent suppression of free speech during wartime from the time of the passage of the Sedition Act of 1798 to the present time.

Roosevelt demands Pelley's silence!

In covering the injustice done Mr. Pelley, Professor Stone initially deals with the frantic and persistent efforts by President Roosevelt to silence him. It became evident that Roosevelt had no qualm in exploiting to the fullest the highest office in the land in silencing his chief antagonist.

The legal avenues for achieving Roosevelt's goal of silencing Mr. Pelley were invoking both the wartime and peacetime "sedition acts," which we have covered in reasonable detail. The wartime sedition act called the Espionage Act of 1917 was the Act under which Mr. Pelley was indicted, tried and sentenced in 1942. The Alien Regulation Act, known as the Smith Act, which Congress passed in 1940, became the peacetime Sedition Act. Mr. Pelley was tried under both Acts with his inclusion in the "Mass Sedition" trial in 1943.

Professor Stone notes the fact that the basic charges in both Acts were the same. The same evidence against Mr. Pelley was presented in both trials. The Constitutional prohibition against "double jeopardy" was flagrantly ignored.

Mr. Pelley opposed the recognition of the Soviet Union and our entrance into WWII. In his piece "Vengeance Under the Law," Pelley's counsel, Mr. McKenzie, cites the many members of Congress, who vehemently opposed the Soviet Union becoming our wartime ally.

When the Soviets broke their Non-aggression Pact, signed on August 23, 1939, with Nazi Germany, miraculously, the bloody hands of Joe Stalin were cleansed over night. We became oblivious to the torture and death of upwards of 10 million in his labor camps.

The Soviet Union became democratic within a fortnight and became our "staunch" ally, fighting for the much-vaunted cause of "democracy." All who opposed such alliance were targeted via the controlled press and the Administration.

Professor Stone cites that in May, 1940, Roosevelt directed J. Edgar Hoover, Attorney General of the United States, to investigate individuals like Mr. Pelley, who opposed the Lend-Lease Program. Roosevelt desperately sought to silence all writers and publishers who were calling public attention to the fact that such Program was a breach of our Neutrality Act. And was literally an act of war.

We were a nation, implementing the Lend Lease Act (enacted on March 11, 1941) shipping contraband of war to England, which were escorted by American destroyers. This was indisputably an act of war that Mr. Pelley, along with leading members of both the House and Senate of the United States, strongly opposed.

My brother, Walt, was arrested for sending post cards to every member of Congress, including the President, opposing the passage of the Lend Lease Act. The federal indictment that followed charged him with sending "threats" through the mail. While a jury quickly acquitted Walt, upholding the citizen's constitutional right to petition elected representatives, this was a clear instance of arrogance in government and an attempt to suppress the will of the sovereign people.

Roosevelt, and his compatriots, despite the overwhelming opposition of the American people, were hell-bent to embroil the nation into WWII.

In January 1942, Roosevelt sent a stringent note to Hoover demanding, "what was being done about William Dudley Pelley!" Two months later, in April, Roosevelt directly confronted Francis Biddle, who had replaced Hoover as Attorney General, and minced no words in wanting to know what was being done about those opposing America's war effort.

He frantically demanded, "When are you going to indict the seditionists." Shortly thereafter the arrests began, with Mr. Pelley singled out as the Administration's prime target.

Perilous Times should be read to get the full impact of how Pelley was fragrantly denied "due process of law" and was the political target of an Administration that was willing to sacrifice the lives of millions to satisfy corporate greed and usurped power.

Chapter Twenty

True Vindication

IT WOULD BE gratifying if we now could draw a line and say that justice has been achieved for Pelley. That after a lifetime of battling for honesty and fair play on all levels of society he had gained a little bit of justice for himself. That truth had finally triumphed.

But the forerunners of Life's Destiny are rarely accorded such recognition in their lifetimes.

Up the centuries true leaders of the people have always been made to endure vilification, persecution, imprisonment, all too frequently death itself. Yet the circumstance of their fate has not been difficult to comprehend. Invariably, each was years ahead of his time and possessed the rare quality of being able to interpret the present in light of the future.

The usurpers of power usually succeed in persecuting and silencing the leader before he can awaken sufficient people in his lifetime to the corruption and exploitation under which they suffer. Always it has been the martyrdom experienced after death that makes the stronger pleading of their cause.

Reflecting on the dynamic leadership of my father-in-law, his activities, his writings, it is evident that his only "crime" was endeavoring to awaken his countrymen to the causes of their dilemmas and the pitfalls that yawned before a nation who blindly trusted its enemies. Time and event have overwhelmingly verified the accuracy of both his exposes and predictions.

The wrongs done Mr. Pelley can never be rectified for him as a person. There is no way that the merciless persecution heaped on him over the many years can be retracted. There is no way that the fifteen years of illegal imprisonment and close surveillance can be restored to him.

123

Frankly, there is no way that rights, which no legitimate power existed in the first place to take away, can be returned!

Vindication?   Even if belatedly, after his death, the courts exonerated him it would not be true vindication. It would only be an admittance of the fact that neither crime nor wrong were committed in the first place.

The only positive way that a leader can be truly vindicated is that the persecution and the imprisonment were not endured in vain. That his efforts were timely and worthwhile. That the people themselves profit from his experience.

If what Pelley's underwent causes the American people to make a new appraisal of their rights, assume their responsibilities, and strive to achieve real peace with economic justice . . .

If what he advocated strengthens others to strive for the goals set down in "No More Hunger" which would restore order, create prosperity and return real sovereignty to the people . . .

If his concern for his fellow human beings will inspire people to love truth and justice for others more than for themselves . . .

Then, and only then, the "Price of Truth" will not have been too high!

Chapter Twenty-one

The Pelley Legacy

THERE WILL BE many appraisals as to Mr. Pelley's lasting legacy to the American people. They will be as diverse as there are varying individuals and groups throughout the land. So much is dependent on what part of his life was of paramount interest to them.

Adelaide and my personal appraisal of the legacy he left for us will surprise, and disappoint, many who followed his dynamic career. Frankly, to us the lasting legacy that he left has nothing to do with his activities dealing with government abuses, the exploitive operations of transnational corporate giants, or even his efforts toward peace with his opposition to Stalinist communism.

Nor has it anything to do with his relentless battle against the abuses of private banking that has been responsible for so much economic injustice and hurt to so many millions of people up the centuries. Nor, not even the toll of unnecessary wars, with such loss of treasure and lives.

In all these critical areas there have been many patriots, along with Mr. Pelley, who have valiantly fought for solutions to the problems and challenges that beset the nation and the world.

His true legacy must be based on two timeless, dynamic and singular concepts that await the people's consideration and comprehension for the balance of this Twenty-first Century.

The real legacy that Mr. Pelley's left us is two-fold:

1. **The blueprinting of a New Economic Order which he called "The Christian Commonwealth" which if embraced by the people would unleash the full productive potential of this nation, provide for an abundant life for every solitary individual, with full implementation of human rights, and the**

achievement of a nation with true economic justice, devoid of debt and violence.

Ultimately, the people will grasp that adversary economic, financial and political systems, like Private Capitalism, have within themselves the seeds for their own destruction. They invariable lead to abusive monopolistic power with an indifference to the tens of millions lacking basic human needs. Only cooperative, teamwork systems can lead to an equitable society within which the people are absolutely sovereign economically and politically.

2. **The second legacy is his writing of over 20 volumes presenting a working philosophy of life which he called "Soulcraft," or craft of the soul, which has helped tens of thousands of people over the years to find ballast, understanding and inspiration in an ever-increasing violent and unstable nation and world.**

These metaphysical teachings are not attempting to supplant Christian teachings. They are instead trying to separate out of them the superstitious dogmas accumulated over the centuries, and make clear many of the allegories and enigmas of ancient scriptures.

Over all, they present a working philosophy of what life is all about, why you are in it, what the purposes are behind adversity, what goals you are achieving, and can achieve, of which you have not yet dared to dream.

* * * * *

It was my good fortunate to write the obituary of my father-in-law for our magazine **The Eagle's Eye** when he made the transition to a Higher Spiritual Plane. The following appeared in the July-August issue, 1965:

126

Chapter Twenty-two

Hail and Farewell!

ON THE NIGHT of June 30, 1965, William Dudley Pelley made his exit from the earthly stage. As he strode into the wings, there came to a close a performance unmatched in dynamism and nobility of purpose. To say that the curtain came down amidst the plaudits of the worldly audience would be to enshroud his role with sentimental unrealism. His was not such a performance.

He was the stormy petrel of the Twentieth Century who valiantly and relentlessly fought every form of subversion. But such was only half his battle. He knew no halfway measures. He fought with equal valor for social change that predatory and abnormal influence might be routed and that there might be ushered in an equitable order governing all human relationships. To such end, he gave his all, unflinchingly and uncompromisingly.

History must record that here was an intellectual giant who had justly earned the garlands of undaunted service to his nation and his fellow human beings. With his release from a physical body that no longer responded to the dictates of his indomitable spirit, the bugle must have sounded loud and clear announcing his arrival into the Halls of the Immortals.

So, hail and farewell, William Dudley Pelley!

Those of us who were nearest to Mr. Pelley knew that only a miracle could have forestalled his transition. Over a period of months he had physically grown weaker. On the morning of June 30th, he lapsed into a deep sleep and the final vigil ensued. He was moved to the local hospital where he was placed under an oxygen tent. At 11:50 pm., he quietly and serenely made the passing.

At his bedside were his wife, his daughter, Adelaide, his grandson, Wink, and this writer, his son-in-law. Our simple prayer, as the Peace of Night enveloped him, was, "Rest well, Pop, you've earned it!"

The next day, as anticipated, a subservient press, radio and TV spewed forth their threadbare and spurious charges. Strong men make strong enemies and even in death no opportunity is foregone to vent venom on those who too effectively indict the seducers and exploiters of humankind.

It is the spleenish ranting of those who fear with a paralyzing fear that unhallowed acts may not be sufficiently camouflaged. It is the villainous calumny of those whose littleness only accentuates the bigness of the man they would crucify.

The Reverend Larry Shaver, a young Methodist minister of our acquaintance, who was familiar with Mr. Pelley's work, gave an inspired sermon. Since most of it was extemporaneous, we have no way of doing justice to the delivery, which by word and intonation reflected reverence and understanding of the life of a great man.

We all felt that Mr. Pelley himself would not have "blue-penciled" a single word that was offered as his final tribute.

His body was buried in Crownland Cemetery in the city of Noblesville.

Certainly, there can be no attempt here to assess the life work and all activities of William Dudley Pelley. He was seventy-five years old when he died and his writings in that span of years fill several bookcases. His contributions to the enlightenment of humankind can only be truly evaluated in the denouement of time and event. However, much that he predicted has already come to pass and, belatedly, increasing numbers of people are recognizing the worth of what he offered for both the material and spiritual liberation of humankind.

Those who have read his book, *No More Hunger,* can appreciate that there can be neither economic well-being nor political sovereignty until the fundamental concepts are embraced by the nation. It was toward realizing this goal that Mr. Pelley championed the rights of every solitary citizen, challenged the most sinister and powerful forces in our society, and advocated those reforms that would underscore the true dignity of humans.

It was this phase of Mr. Pelley's work that subjected him to every abuse and persecution that the enemies of humankind could contrive and execute. Such a stand was "sedition" to those in power, whether in peace or war, and for it he was forced to endure seven and a half years of illegal imprisonment.

Millions of people, especially of a past era, are familiar with Mr. Pelley's career as a nationally known fiction writer. They have read and enjoyed the two hundred and forty-eight short stories that were published in such magazines as **Saturday Evening Post, Red Book** and **The American Magazine.** They are equally familiar with his full-length novels, two of which were made into movies, and know of his writing a score of movie scenarios.

Many people are primarily acquainted with Mr. Pelley through over a score of his books penetrating through the dogma and crystallization of orthodox religious thinking, giving bewildered humanity a fresh glimpse into the essence of all life. To them the beauty and the dynamism of the whole Liberation-Soulcraft Doctrine is the fact that it encompasses an arena of human functioning wherein no mortal is indispensable, yet, *"every life, no matter how humble, no matter how tragic, no matter how broken and thwarted, hath a meaning and an inner glory and is precious in His sight."*

In such enlightenment, they have found ballast in confronting life, they have found spiritual increment in all experience, and they have found unshakeable faith in a purposeful and good Universe.

Even Mr. Pelley's worst enemies would have to concede that he lived a full and active life. There was no arena of human thought, or human endeavor, to which he failed to apply both his hand and insatiable mind. He left a legacy immeasurable for oncoming generations.

We, who were nearest to Mr. Pelley, know that he would not want us to be either overly sentimental or grief-burdened at his passing. This would be inconsistent with the man's own philosophy and the understanding he has imparted to us. Dying is as natural as being born and the thing that counts is how we have displayed ourselves in the interim. Life is the testing ground of spirit to see how it measures up in compassionate service to others.

It is in this context that the Prince of Peace must have raised His hand in blessing and said, "William Dudley Pelley, noble servant, thy job well done!"

---Melford Pearson

* * * * *

At the end of volume **Seven Minutes in Eternity,** Adelaide wrote a concluding piece entitled "The Road Ahead." Her insight focusing on the future is most relevant to be included in this book.

Chapter Twenty-three

The Road Ahead

As WE COME to the end of this small volume, I would like to add a word of my own about the present status of the Liberation-Soulcraft work begun by my father as a result of the "Seven Minutes" experience, and share with you a speculation on its future.

There is an old argument, as I know you are aware, as to how the world may be saved from its own folly. The religionists insist that only by conversion of the individual heart, will this end be accomplished. No amount of individual conversion can take place say the social reformers, until the outside pressures that crush, distort and maim the human heart are removed.

It is one of the great appeals of the Liberation-Soulcraft Doctrine that is places equal emphasis on both the individual and the group. Neither can function properly nor fulfill its purpose without the other. No man exists in a vacuum; no group exists without the individuals who compose it. It is the purpose of the individual spirit to grow and expand, but it is in its relationship and service to others that such growth and expansion most rapidly takes place.

When my father began his real lifework after the "Seven Minutes" experience, he called the wave of nationwide interest that sprang up, the Liberation Movement. He was then concerned with the purposes and vicissitudes of the individual human spirit, breaking up outmoded and crystallized concepts of religion and opening new corridors and vistas of freedom for aspiring humanity. This was Liberation of the Spirit.

But then he went on into practical application of these principles to everyday life and work, challenging the Powers That Be in their greedy domination of the minds, bodies and property of their fellows. This was Liberation of the Human

Being. Such challenging quite naturally brought forth reprisals from those attacked, locking him behind iron bars for seven and a half years.

The restrictions under which he found himself when released caused him to concentrate solely upon finishing the job of setting down the spiritual philosophy, which he now called Soulcraft, and making it into books to be read and absorbed by oncoming generations.

It was in the face of these restrictions upon his activity that my husband, Melford, and I, with my father's help, organized Aquila Press, Inc. for the main purpose of promoting and furthering the economic ideas he had first set down in the book, *No More Hunger.* Thus the stream had been forced to divide into two branches, although fed by the same source.

After the passing of my father, my stepmother carried on the promotion of the Soulcraft books, while Aquila continued to promote the concept of the Cooperative Commonwealth. But the passing last year of my stepmother also, the two streams ran together once again. For business purposes we must keep the two branches separate at least for the present, but the goals and intentions of promoting the total Liberation-Soulcraft work are one.

Fellowship Press, Inc. will continue to print and publish all Soulcraft books, and Aquila will continue to print and publish *No More Hunger,* and all material dealing with political and economic reform.

And now, what is the promise of the future?

Even though it has been all of forty years since I first heard my father mention the coming of the Aquarian Age and the beginning birth pangs that would be attendant on an event of such magnitude, even though he and we have suffered many a disappointment and much heartache as the years swing by, there has never been a marked deviation from the fundamental direction of the work since it all began that night in May, 1928.

Not only is this corroborated by our own observation and common sense, and a lifetime of study and research, but also there is in addition a potent prophecy to which I would call your attention, that provides a guideline for his whole life.

On an evening in August 1929, in New York City, my father received a message. He has written it up in several places, but I will quote from his autobiography, *The Door to Revelation*, mimeographed edition, written in 1935 and now long out of print.

"On or about October 15th of this year, there is coming a crash upon the bourses of the world that will pull down all peoples into seven years of famine.

"Within a year or thereabout you will find yourself at the head of a great spiritual movement that shall spread across this nation. But that is not of account, since it only prepares the minds of certain leaders to step from the mass and proceed to function with you.

"In three years or thereabouts, you will find yourself at the head of a national vigilante organization, a quasi-military force, which you will project and bring to strange flower. But not as men might hope. Not as you yourself might conceive at its inception.

"As that climax approaches, you will write a great book. It will show the frenzied and harassed human race how a better order may be realized, how evil can be curbed, how life's dark master forces shall be circumscribed themselves and ultimately fought to ruin.

"Nine years it will; be your commission to lead in the installation of this greater economic order, as the Golden Age comes in. On March 4, 1945, your political labors will be finished. Thereafter, if you have served as you are expected,

133

seventeen years will be permitted you . . . to set up those institutions for spiritual explorations that now seem enticing pastime."

How such interpretation is needed?

The first is devious. The second is the Soulcraft movement whose spiritual principles should be understood by any leader. The third refers to the Silver Legion, definitely and finally dissolved by my father in the spring of 1940. The fourth has to be *No More Hunger,* the only one of his books to fit the description. In regard to the fifth, the facts are there even though vastly different from early interpretation.

In March, 1943 my father's political work was indeed finished as the sudden death of the judge brought the infamous Mass Sedition Trial to an end. Chief Justice Laws ruled it would be a "travesty on justice" to continue the trial, so, in a sense, my father's political career ended in exoneration although his imprisonment was prolonged.

And a final note: His last publication bore the date of June, 1962.

It was my father's brevet in this life to initiate the Liberation-Soulcraft movement, and because of his special talent in communication, to set down the full delineation of a philosophy befitting a new dispensation, the Aquarian Age.

Although the physical accomplishment of the goals did not occur while he was still on this side of life, both the goals and the guidelines for reaching them glow brighter with every passing day.

From whatever loftier plane my father may be watching, we can be sure he is pleading that we open our minds and hearts to the great and simple truths taught by the Carpenter who is the Architect of the Ages:

"Do ye no ungodly thing that godliness may prosper; do ye all merciful things that righteousness may prosper. Put

134

from yourselves those errors that are childish, take unto yourselves the armors of true wisdom. . . . Give of yourselves to your utmost farthings that the world may rise up in years to mature and call your names blessed in that ye didst sing a song of redemption for the unfortunate who had not your voicings, or your longings, or your seeings. . . ."

---Adelaide Pelley Pearson

I want to make the final chapter of this book an excerpt from Mr. Pelley's book **Thresholds of Tomorrow.** The message conveyed is pertinent and timely and gives us a poignant glimpse into the soul and mind of the author who fought so gallantly for a better world.

Chapter Twenty-four

We Are Set Upon A Mighty Journey. .

A NEW BIRTH of Spirituality and Brotherhood is coming in these United States such, as the previous world has never known!

A spiritual Renaissance is coming that is due to sweep America!

Men are suddenly to realize that they are eternal beings, that all these dramas and woes are merely passing phases of their mortal education, that out of the welter and wrack of them is coming a New Earth, conducted under new principles, principles that first found utterance on the shores of Galilee nineteen centuries in the past.

This is Christ's Republic!

Friends, we're citizens of that Republic . . . in more then one way. We've gotten ourselves born as citizens into it, to live through these times of its Second Birth and be shareholders and pioneers in the installation of a true Christian Commonwealth! Catch that picture, and keep it in your consciousness!

A new birth of spirituality! Take note of that also!

What is Spirituality?

Spirituality means the Indomitable Essence of which the Eternal Man is composed, lifting him and bearing him above every barrier of opposition and discouragement that mortal life holds or can produce, causing him to recognize something more to Consciousness than merely facing the slings and arrows of outrageous fortune and bringing him out triumphant over circumstances because he discerns that such is God's way of polishing and mounting the jewel called Character.

Spirituality supplies man with a far throw on his destiny, the panoramic picture of why he's temporarily in mortality, what he retains from it to serve him up the ages. The materialist laughs scornfully that there is such thing, because he hasn't yet arrived at a consciousness of its potentials in his own right. But those in whom Spirituality is developed and galvanic have armor and an armament that nothing can successfully assail or take away.

Think of the episodes in history when Spirituality has risen victorious over the ruins and wreckage of secular realities. I don't need to call your attention to the long roster of sublime souls who faced their deaths in the Roman arena for their faith in the Ultimate Mission of the Elder Brother, Jesus, the Christ.

I think of specific instances like Joan of Arc, an illiterate peasant girl "hearing voices" in a pleasant garden in Lorraine. Insane as it seemed, Indomitable Spirit sent her to audience with the king himself, who clad her in shining armor, and put her at the head of his legions.

Indomitable Spirit in shining armor!

What has the sodomic materialist given to match it?

So she rode at the head of her monarch's columns, a Maid Triumphant, infusing new life in the spirits of fighters even though the ending of the drama brought her to the stake. What did the English burn but her poor body? Spirit went ON and on triumphant! Indomitable Spirit in Shining Armor could ride on transcendent to the very crackling fires of hell itself! . . . That Joan *rode* is the thing. . . .

Think of other immortal episodes up through history where Indomitable Spirit has vanquished everything secular before it. Captain James Lawrence, mortally wounded, knowing he was dying on his own shattered quarterdeck, lifting himself up on an elbow and having only one thought, not of his own sacrifice but of the American Navy whose unconquerable spirit he represented, crying to his seamen as parting adjuration, "Don't give up the ship!"

Think of Stephen Decatur, hero of the sea fight off Tripoli, crying out these immortal words: "Our country! In her intercourse with foreign nations may she always be in the right; but our country, right or wrong!"

Think of John Stark at the Battle of Bennington, viewing the outnumbering ranks of the hired Hessians of the British and crying in majestic valor, "There they are boys! Tonight they're ours or Molly Stark sleeps a widow!" Spirit Indomitable! That night the Hessian mercenaries were ours, and Molly Stark in due time had her husband restored to her.

SPIRIT can do anything once it sets its mind to it. What kind of renegades have we, the progeny of such stalwarts, turned out to be, that we can't stand firm as rocks in a sea of vacillation and petty purpose and let Invincible Spirit send forth the glory-cry, "one with God is a Majority!"

Suppose we give more thought to the power of Spirit, rightly conceived and embraced, to carry us indefatigably through the crisis that looms and set the world rightside up again, not in the manner of leaving it to Holy Spirit to clean up the debris we may have made of our blessings, but in the manner of recognizing that there is a great cross-section of us who have come into life to show mankind how this debris may be cleaned away by putting lambent Spirituality to the fore, and solving our quandaries by more practical application of the Eternal Verities.

Remember, this nation wasn't founded at the behest of Great Intellects and then brought to actuality by the superb heroisms of Great Stalwarts, to have a life in the world of 186 years and then forever perish.

I take the position that we have only begun our true history as a Republic, and whatever has happened and gone has been little but preparation for that which is still ahead.

139

We as a country are upon a mighty journey. We have traversed only a few infants' miles of it yet. It proceeds across oceans and up continents of Splendor. Let us be spiritually ready for it, for only by Spirit shall we grasp the magnificence of it. . . .

* * * * *

The prime resource of Mr. Pelley's beliefs and activities are the many books that he wrote. Many of them have been referred to in the pages of this book. In 2001 a "Publishing and Copyright Agreement" was made with **Soulcraft Enterprises** *to print, promote and sell his esoteric books. Comprehensive information can be obtained on the Internet by logging on to "Soulcraftteachings.com"*

The following short bibliography is to present books that give insight and background to Mr. Pelley's ideas and activities.

Bibliography

Adams, Silas Walter *The Legalized Crime of Banking,* Meador Publishing Co. Boston, 1958

Beard, Charles A. *An Economic Interpretation of the Constitution of the United States,* Macmillan, 1961

Beard, Charles A. *President Roosevelt and the Coming of the War, 1941* Yale University Press, New Haven, 1948

Bloom, Allen *The Closing of the American Mind,* Simon & Schuster, NY, 1987

Congressional Union of Scotland *MONEY—A Christian View,* Glasgow, 1962

Declaration of Independence

Dwinell, Olive Cushing *The Story of Our Money,* Meador, Boston, 1946

Ellis, Joseph J. *Founding Fathers,* Alfred A. Knopf, 2000

Findley, Paul *They Dare to Speak Out,* Lawrence Hill & Co, Connecticut

Fuller, R. Buckminster *Utopia or Oblivion, the Prospects for Humanity,* Bantam Books, 1971

Greider, William *Who Will Tell the People,* Simon & Schuster, 1992

Herman & Chomsky *Manufacturing Consent,* Pantheon Books, 1988

Kennedy, Edward E. *The Fed and the Farmer,* published by Edward Kennedy, Pismo Beach, California

King, Martin Luther, Jr. *Where Do We Go From Here, Chaos or Community,* Beacon Press, Boston, 1967

Lernoux, Penny *In Banks We Trust,* Penguin Books, 1984

Lindbergh, Charles A. *Autobiography of Values,* Harcourt Brace Jovanovich, NY, 1977

Locke, John *Treatise on Government*

Mills, C. Wright *The Power Elite,* Oxford University Press, 1959

Mills. C. Wright *The Causes of World War Three,* Simon & Schuster, NY, 1958

Morton, Frederic *The Rothschild's, A Family Portrait,* Curtis (Atheneum) New York, 1962

Paine, Thomas *The Rights of Man*

Russell, Bertrand *Political Ideals,* Simon & Schuster, 1964

Soddy, Frederic *Wealth, Virtual Wealth and Debt,* Omni Publications, Hawthorne, CA 1961

Sorokin, Pitirim and Walter Lunden, *Power and Morality,* Porter Sargent, Boston, 1959

Stone, Geoffrey R. *Perilous Times,* W. W. Norton, NY and London, 2004

The Report of the National Advisory Commission on Civil Disorders (The Kerner Report) E. P. Dutton & Co. NY, 1968

Thoren and Warner *The Truth in Money Book,* Truth in Money Incorporated, Chagrin Falls, Ohio, 1984

Vickers, Vincent C. *Economic Tribulation,* Omni Publications, Hawthorne, California, 1960

Voorhis, Jerry *Out of Debt, Out of Danger*

Zinn, Howard *Declaration of Independence,* Harper Collins, NY, 1990

* * * * *

Hearings before the Sub-Committee on Domestic Finance, of the Committee on Banking and Currency, House of Representatives, Eighty-Eighth Congress, Second Session on the **Federal Reserve System After Fifty Years** *(3 volumes, 1964)* **A Primer on Money** *(1964)* **Money Facts** *(1964)*

Federal Reserve Directors: A Study of Corporate and Banking Influence *by the Committee on Banking and Currency and Housing , House of Representatives, 94th Congress, Second Session, August, 1976*

Interlocking Directorates Among the Major U. S. Corporations, *by Subcommittee on Reports, Accounting and Management, Committee on Governmental Affairs, United States Senate, January, 1978*

Index

143

144

145

On November 11, 2005 Adelaide graduated to a Higher Spiritual Plane.

Mel, 92 years young, resides with his feline partner, "Reeka," in Noblesville, Indiana, and is currently working on two books, *Scourge of Cords* and *A Reluctant Heretic.*